S0-AAA-631

Intelligent Fear

Intelligent Fear

HOW TO MAKE FEAR WORK FOR YOU

Michael Clarkson

Marlowe & Company
New York

INTELLIGENT FEAR: *How to Make Fear Work for You*
Copyright © Michael Clarkson 2002, 2003

Published by
Marlowe & Company
An Imprint of Avalon Publishing Group Incorporated
161 William Street, 16th Floor
New York, NY 10038

Originally published in Canada by Key Porter Books Limited. This edition
published by arrangement.

All rights reserved. No part of this book may be reproduced in whole or in part without written
permission from the publisher, except by reviewers who may quote brief excerpts in connection
with a review in a newspaper, magazine, or electronic publication; nor may any part of this book
be reproduced, stored in a retrieval system, or transmitted in any form or by any means electronic, mechanical, photocopying, recording, or other, without written permission from the
publisher.

Library of Congress Control Number: 2002117470
ISBN 1-56924-489-8

9 8 7 6 5 4 3 2 1
Designed by Peter Maher
Printed in the United States of America
Distributed by Publishers Group West

Contents

To my sons Paul and Kevin Clarkson, with love and healthy fear.

Acknowledgments

The thesis of this book and the strategies it recommends sometimes take an original form, but of course any author/researcher who embarks on such a complex journey as fear management is indebted to others who have gone before.

Thank you to such deep thinkers in this field as Walter B. Cannon, Hans Selye, Herbert Benson, Robert S. Eliot, Massad Ayoob, James E. Loehr, Arnold Fox, Mihaly Csikszentmihalyi, Daniel Goleman, Ned Hallowell, Peter Hanson, Gloria Witkin, Robert Nideffer, and Robert Thayer—many of whom granted me interviews.

Thank you to my wife Jennifer and my sons Paul and Kevin for following my winding career, and to my parents Irene and Fred Clarkson and in-laws Tony and Kathleen Vanderklei for their support.

Anna Porter, the editors at Key Porter Books and my agent, Robert Mackwood of Contemporary Communications, have also been invaluable to me.

Thanks, as well, to the daily newspapers I have worked for, including my present employer the *Toronto Star*, and to my first book publisher, Human Kinetics, for publishing my earlier stories and works of psychology.

Introduction:
Training Your Fears

"Fear is intelligence. Fear keeps you alert. Fear is a built-in mechanism for performance ... control it and you can become a star."
—former National Hockey League star Derek Sanderson, now a TV broadcaster

While reporting for a newspaper on a National Basketball Association game in Los Angeles, I found myself about to lose a game within a game.

Deadline was minutes away and I was not even close to finishing my story about Magic Johnson's comeback. As several hundred other reporters struggled to complete their own work in the elbow-to-elbow media room, I felt myself tense up. My fingers trembled on the keyboard, and I could hear my heart above the rumble of the crowd in the Great Western Forum. I was afraid of missing deadline for the first time in my journalism career.

Fortunately, I had a last-minute strategy. I got angry with myself. How could I allow my newspaper to finance a 3,000-mile journey so that I could screw up and embarrass myself? "Dammit," I muttered. "Just do your job."

Usually mild mannered, I became aggressive for a fleeting moment. Then, I poured that anger into fashioning the story and typing it into my computer. Swiftly, my counter-productive fear became mobilized into potent energy. My new mindset produced some natural magic, turning toxic levels of adrenaline—which had flooded my mind and body in response to the fear I had been feeling—into a more manageable cocktail of the proactive hormones dopamine and noradrenaline.

Now it was my story, rather than my heart, that was thumping. I thought and typed faster than normal, and finished the 1,000-word piece with one minute to spare—even after trips to the teams' dressing rooms for interviews and a glance at Magic's trademark smile.

While I can't biologically prove what transpired that night, I *know* that it happened because I have been studying this type of phenomena since 1988. Back then, I covered an inquest in which an Ontario Provincial Police officer reported a weird experience during a gun battle—he claimed that the heated action became a twilight zone experience as the suspect seemed to turn around slowly, giving him more time to react and defend himself. An "expert" witness called this phenomenon the "tachy psyche effect"—which I have since discovered is actually *tachypsychia*, a Greek work for "speed of the mind." He explained that, during threatening moments, the mind and body go into a defensive arousal mode, summoning powerful hormones at a frightening pace and providing increased resources to deal with the situation. I was intrigued, and like any reporter who smells a story, I started investigating. Over the years, I have become a strange combination of research scientist, interpreter, and lab rat, dissecting fear from several angles and finding ways to harness it.

I have learned that our greatest achievements and our greatest failures often have the same root—fear. It is how we manage the *energy* of fear—the rush of powerful hormones in pressure situations—that will decide our fate. We fail when our fear reaction interferes with our performance, as it was doing during my deadline crunch in Los Angeles. On the other hand, if we can channel this same *fear energy* directly into our work, we can flourish like we have never done.

In fact, many unexplained phenomena are products of fear energy, including "in-the-zone" experiences at work and in sports, accidents which seem to happen in slow motion, time distortions in deadline situations, and feats in which people succeed despite being ill or injured.

And yet, most of us perform poorly when nervous. Too often, our *emergency fear system*—which we activate many times a day in the form of excitement or distress—kicks in at unmanageable levels and we don't know how to handle it. In the sports and business worlds, this is known as choking. (The term has a biological basis; it's derived from a Greek word meaning "a narrowing of the esophagus," which can occur during high arousal. More often than not, students recall their studies better when they are not being tested, police officers shoot more accurately on the practice range than in gun battles and athletes are at their best before a match nears its dramatic end.

When it comes to fear, we're not very intelligent. We don't know why we choke, or why we get stressed. We don't realize that fear is causing our tension—or if we do, we're afraid to admit it. Have you ever felt nervous before an important job or an interview? Does facing your boss make you tense? You are probably relieved when (and if) these sensations go away. But what if you could welcome these feelings? What if you could use them to your advantage? You can. Fear was intended to help you *overcome* threatening situations—and for a small percentage of people in the corporate and sports worlds it does. These men and women are able to continually defeat their opposition and their deadlines because they've learned how to train their fears.

After interviewing hundreds of high achievers—from basketball icon Michael Jordan to CNN founder Ted Turner to golfing great Nancy Lopez—I have come to a sad conclusion: they often stumble onto their secrets through trial and error. Until now, there have been few organized plans for harnessing fear. Although there are countless strategies and self-help books on how to control stress and ease pressure, I believe we need to concentrate on the underlying cause—fear. Until we start seeing stress and pressure as very natural fear responses, we will continue to have problems. Until we realize that grace under pressure is actually fear management, only a small percentage of people will succeed.

While observing stressful situations as a police reporter, investigative journalist and top amateur athlete, I have discovered numerous examples of our fear reaction and ways to harness it. In ten years of writing at one newspaper, I was told I did not miss deadline.

In sports, I have evoked altered states that have allowed me to perform almost perfectly "in the zone." And in 1999, as my wife was drowning in the swimming pool of the cruise ship *Westerdam*, I saved her with my mind. A poor swimmer who is afraid of water, I somehow managed to employ the emotional techniques I had been studying as part of my research for this book. I shifted all of my energy and resources away from my helpless wife and focused instead on the physical technique of swimming to save her. It worked. Only when Jennifer was recovering in a hospital bed on the ship did I realize that one of my theories had been right all along: you can turn your fear into a pro-ductive force, even a life-saving one. Later that night, as the buzz got around the ship, well-wishers wondered how a skinny, out-of-shape fifty-one-year-old who could hardly swim had managed to pull it off. At the time, I could not explain my technique. Now, I know that through simple thought, I allowed my emergency fear system to perform its impressive duty without interference.

I am not a hero. I have simply learned—through observation, trial and error—how to make the most out of my body's fear reaction. In the pages that follow, I will outline and explain the three strategies that have helped me achieve this goal. You, too, can evoke these powers, in situations not only on the edge of catastrophe, but at work and at home.

The strategies are not complicated: in fact, you may use some of them already. But in order to successfully work with fear, we need to employ them con-sistently and in sync with one another. These are the three strategies:

1. **Awareness:** Recognizing and admitting your feelings of fear and how much they affect you and your work. Recognizing where the fear comes from, and that it is often related to the defense of your ego and pride.
2. **Management:** Keeping fear and pressure at manageable levels through attitude and better use of your resources.
3. **Focus:** Dealing with high-pressure situations through focusing and chan-neling techniques.

I believe that everyone can benefit from an exploration of the three strategies—from people facing pressure situations or competition at work (police officers, lawyers, stockbrokers, or business executives, amateur or pro-fessional athletes) to those facing interviews or exams to those caught in a physical confrontation or in the stress of everyday life.

As I offer these strategies to deal with pressure in many lines of work, I will also include stories from rescuers, corporate winners, and everyday heroes from across North America.

Fear management remains a young science, but we are making progress. Please join me on this exciting journey.

I
Awareness

This section features an analysis of both fear and our
reaction to it. It includes background information about
our two fear systems—the emergency fear system and the
worry system. Chapters 1 and 2 offer insights into what
fear is, where it comes from and how the threats we feel
are now professional and social, rather than physical.
Chapter 3 deals with the effects of fear and pressure on
you and your work.

1
Understanding Fear

"Fear, in evolution, has a special prominence: perhaps more than any other emotion, it is crucial for survival."
—Daniel Goleman, author of *Emotional Intelligence*

In this new millennium of fast-paced living and increased pressures, we need strategies for working under pressure. Our fear reaction—hardwired into our mind-bodies millions of years ago—has become outdated and confused.

Just the other night, my phone rang at 3:14 A.M. I sat up and fumbled for the receiver. Holy mackerel, were my kids out? Was someone in dire straits? I'd only been awake for 2.5 seconds and already I was sweating. My heart was pounding. "H-h-hello?" From my sudden strength, the phone went flying across the room. "Oh, sorry," said the voice at the other end. "I thought this was Five-O Taxi ..."

Boy, did he get a wrong number. And, boy, did my sympathetic nervous system get a wrong number. Has this ever happened to you? If it has, it proves a point. We may not be cave people anymore, but physically, we still react to danger and potential danger the same way we have for more than a million years.

Once you get over the fright of a false alarm, this living and breathing link to our ancestors of the deep past is kind of neat. For a moment, we can feel what they felt like when confronted by a behemoth. This fear was intelligently designed for mostly physical threats, but, of course, reacting like this day after day is what causes us distress, and often lousy work performance.

When faced with a threat, we still get a pounding heart, a sweating brow, and more powerful muscles. And yet the things we react to, the things we are threatened by, have changed considerably because the things which establish the threats—our needs and priorities—have altered, as well. We don't use spiked clubs anymore; we use golf clubs. And instead of defending ourselves physically, we defend our ego and pride. And yet, how many of us are aware of our reactions?

When you are in a rush shaving in the morning, you may feel your hand trembling slightly. Maybe you are afraid of being late and having the boss raise his eyebrows? When you are driving and you suddenly feel your fingers tightly grip the steering wheel, that's fear, too. At work, if you become angry at a co-workers' laziness and you feel the hairs rising on the back of your neck, readying you for a confrontation, your anger has a fear base. When someone irritably raises a voice in the classroom, ditto. In fact, most anger, tension, and nervousness are rooted in fear—our reaction to danger—according to Robert E. Thayer, a psychology professor at California State University, Long Beach, and a leading authority on emotions.

We react through worry and fear more than we react through love or happiness. Whether we know it or not, fear is as much a part of our lives as eating and breathing. "Fear is at the core of our human experience—more than joy, anger, sadness, and even love," says Edward M. Hallowell, a Boston psychiatrist and author of several books on worry. "Every cell in our body and each of our physiological systems can contribute in one way or another to our fear response."

In order for us to survive, nature has equipped us with numerous incredible systems of defense against outside threats—from the immune system which protects us from disease to eyelashes which close 20,000 times a day to repel dirt. Even sexual attraction and the subsequent sexual arousal are types of defense systems, designed by nature to keep us procreating. We also boast a powerful fear defense system, which alerts us to a wide range of threats—from an assailant on the street to an important project at work to concerns over our children. This fear system has two forms: long-term worry and short-term emergency fear.

The Emergency Fear System

Emergency fear is our knee-jerk reaction to a sudden threat, whether it is a car crash, a mugger, a golfing opponent, or a public speaking engagement. To deal with these threats, we have the emergency fear system, which is capable of small miracles, of defending lives, of wreaking havoc. We are all rigged with such a piece of equipment, but some people turn it on more than others. When it is activated again and again for the wrong reasons, it causes distress, tension, poor work performance, and even illness.

Sadly, we often neglect the benefits of the emergency fear system because we don't know how to tap its substantial powers. In fact, we may not even be aware that it exists. Or we may be slightly aware of it from time to time, but don't do anything about its results. The encouraging news is that your emergency fear system can save your life or the lives of others. In Drumheller, Alberta, nineteen-year-old Derrick Wilson rushed to the aid of his uncle Dale, who was knocked unconscious when a crop-duster airplane crashed into a wheat field. Wilson tore a heavy, jammed seatbelt apart with his hands, freeing the slumped victim. "I ripped it apart like Scotch Tape," he said. "I wouldn't have been able to do that other times."

Under intense conditions at work, your emergency fear system can heighten your attention and production. Unfortunately, we have been conditioned to believe that anything to do with fear is to be avoided at all costs. We must change this way of thinking. It is the way we *cope* with fear which needs improving. "What most people fail to realize is that whether you are facing a big business deal, a showdown with the boss, or a couple of muggers, you will feel fear," says Geoff Thompson, an expert of crisis situations. "We have to help people break down the prison walls by educating people in the histrionics of fear; how to recognize, understand, and subsequently control and/or employ fear as an ally."

The emergency fear system has been around since the dawn of time, and we are just finding ways to adapt it to modern life. Whenever you feel threatened—physically, mentally, professionally, or socially—your mind and body go through a series of complex and immediate changes to help you to cope. Depending on the severity of the threat, or what you think of the threat, here are some of the possible biochemical changes, which I refer to as arousal:

- Your heart goes from pumping one gallon of blood per minute to pumping up to five gallons per minute.
- Pupils dilate for maximum visual perception.
- Blood is rerouted away from skin and internal organs toward brain and skeletal muscles. Your muscles tense and you feel stronger.
- Arteries constrict for maximum pressure to pump blood to the heart and other muscles.
- The adrenal gland is activated to pump cortisol (it maintains pupil dilation and artery constriction by stimulating the formation of hormones).
- Fatty acids are produced and your liver converts glycogen into glucose to provide extra energy.
- Breathing becomes more rapid and nostrils flare, causing an increased supply of air.
- The digestive system is shut down and vessels to the skin and kidneys are constricted.
- Pain threshold increases. In case of injury, blood clots faster, ready to repair damage to your arteries.
- An increase in blood cholesterol allows for long-distance fuel.

Whew! You can feel some of the changes in the form of a sudden queasiness in your stomach, or a tension in your neck or shoulders, or sudden bout of quick breathing or sweating. If a threat is serious enough, you may feel nausea, the shakes, and a sudden loss of power or confidence. Conversely, if you accept this fear reaction properly, you may feel physically and mentally powerful and totally in control.

At its height, the emergency fear system produces a response known as fight or flight, with all the bells and whistles, including hormones such as adrenaline (as potent as rocket fuel) and endorphin (a greater painkiller than morphine). When you are faced with death, fight or flight offers you superior strength, speed, and concentration to help you stay alive. But your mind-body does not reach this heightened state of arousal for every threat. If we rate the mind-body response on a scale of 1 to 5, fight or flight would be a 5 while a 1 response would arise from a relatively mild threat, such as a business meeting with a stranger. People who are more highly strung will tend to have a higher than normal response to each situation. As we will see later, it is also possible to elevate your arousal threshold in order to take advantage of the added power it bestows.

When the mind-body goes into an arousal state, it is just the first of three potential "stages of stress." If the arousal stage is high or long-lasting, the mind-body goes into a second, or resistance, phase in which it adjusts to the arousal. If the arousal continues, the third and final stage would be exhaustion.

Early researchers coined the phrase "fight or flight" because

A Sample of Mind-Body Alarms

1 Alarm: Nervous system on alert.
2 Alarm: A phone call in the middle of the night.
3 Alarm: A quarrel at work or at home.
4 Alarm: A threat to your ego or pride during competition or at work.
5 Alarm: A physical threat or an extreme threat to ego or self-esteem.

they believed that, when confronted with a serious threat, animals and human beings generally reacted by fighting or running away. As research continued, another way of dealing with a threat was discovered—freezing in your tracks to make you less conspicuous to a predator. Like flight, this is sometimes confused with panic (and sometimes it is panic), but freezing has a definite use of its own; it gives you a chance to assess options in the face of danger. Some researchers called this fright and expanded the phrase to "fight, flight or fright."

I offer a fourth response—faking. I suggest that in our arousal responses to a threat, we fake a fight as much as we fight, flee, or freeze. And nature offers evidence—primitive man was covered with hairs, which would rise up on his body, making him look bigger prior to a potential confrontation with an enemy or a predator. That's the ultimate fake. (The hair-standing-on-end phenomenon is still reported today. Olympic athletes such as Britain's Daley Thompson and golfing great Nancy Lopez have said their hairs stand on end when they are psyched up.)

Fear Reactions

Hormone	Purpose	How It's Triggered
dopamine	The body's rocket fuel, from which many other hormones follow. It stimulates aggression and awareness, coordinates muscle movement, and speeds up thinking.	From challenge. It responds to positive thinking more than adrenaline does and speeds up momentum.
adrenaline	Increases heart and respiration rates, widens air passages, increases blood pressure and muscle tension. But it's overrated and often capable of more harm than good.	Mostly through fear and sometimes anger. It's more of a defensive "flight" fuel.
noradrenaline	Similar to adrenaline in increasing heart rate and muscle activity. Improves alertness and reaction time. Strengthens willpower.	When a person turns to aggression in a competitive situation. It's more of a "fight" fuel than adrenaline.
testosterone	A fight, but not a flight response, bringing strength, speed, and power to maximum levels. Enhances the will to dominate an opponent.	Through a very competitive mindset and strong desire to overcome another person.

Hormone	Purpose	How It's Triggered
cortisol	A long-term hormone that prolongs adrenaline and noradrenaline and adds energy. High levels can damage brain cells and accelerate aging.	Released when a person feels anxiety, anger, guilt, frustration.
DHEA	Promotes well-being and joy and reduces anxiety. Gives added energy.	Released in the endocrine system by positive, loving thoughts. People sometimes raise it with thoughts of loved ones at time of crisis.
serotonin	The neurotransmitter of inner peace. Linked with self-esteem, confidence, and the ability to concentrate. Creates relaxation and happiness.	Appreciative feelings toward others. Stretching, walking, low-impact aerobics, and meditative martial arts boost its levels.
endorphin	A powerful painkiller, produced by the hypothalamus in the brain, it's the body's natural morphine. Suspected as the producer of runner's high.	Triggered by laughter, pain and other intense feelings.
oxytocin	Promotes social bondage and team work.	Thinking of achievements and goals in a team rather than individual sense.

Worry: Your Other Fear System

This book focuses mainly on emergency fear, but worry is important because it often interacts with emergency fear and influences the way we react to a threat or to pressure. When an immediate threat comes up, the intensity of our response may be influenced by how much we have already been worrying (and getting aroused) about the potential for the threat. If we have been worrying about downsizing for some time, for example, we may start to shake or sweat when the boss calls us into his office.

The reverse can also be true: our long-term worry can be affected by a short-term emergency fear reaction. For example, I have a history of going faint—which is a form of emergency fear response—when I go to the doctor or dentist. Because of my potential embarrassing reaction at a medical office, I avoid trips to the doctor or dentist. Thus, my long-term worry is produced by my short-term fear reaction.

Just as emergency fear employs the emergency fear system as its major resource, worry has the worry system. And the worry system keeps us busy. Each of us has about 66,000 thoughts a day, two-thirds of them worries. To enable us to respond, this system has quite a broad range of resources—more elaborate and thought out than those of the emergency fear system, which primarily uses fear and anger. Certainly, fear is at the base of the worry system, but other emotions have time and chance to seep into the potent mix, including love, sadness, jealousy, and hope. Worry often uses the hormone cortisol, which has a number of benefits and can stay in your system for weeks or months; but it can also make you ill you if worry too much. When we worry (constructively) about an upcoming event, we can call upon our energy, willpower, talent, and strategy.

"Worry was intended to be a useful, built-in alarm system," says Edward M. Hallowell. "Not all worry is bad. Effective planning depends on anticipating danger. This is worry at its best. The trick is to learn to worry well, at the right time, to the right degree."

"Worry is a valuable and natural emotion, a helpful asset," write marketing consultants Michael Gill and Sheila Patterson in their book *Fired Up!* "They always tell you in corporate life: 'Don't worry about it.' And that is good advice when you are still inside the corporate zoo. But when you become an entrepreneur, you are flying your own plane and worry becomes one of your most important ways to succeed. When you start to worry, remember this fact: Fear is the fuel that makes the entrepreneurial person a success."

Emotional Drive

Within the worry system is an important resource which I call emotional drive. Simply put, it is our will to survive. In the broadest sense, it is life itself—without it, there is not much point having muscles and other physical defenses. Some people may call this determination. We are determined to survive, so we do whatever it takes, and the human species has certainly proven formidable in the face of many serious threats over the centuries. I believe emotional drive is often activated through healthy worry.

This emotional drive, which is fueled by fear, is also set up for us to evolve as human beings, says researcher Rush W. Dozier Jr. "Fear, and the satisfaction we experience in overcoming it, is also a constructive force. It helps give us our drive, dynamism, maturity, and depth. If we lived only for pleasure, we as a species might lapse into a contented, stultifying stagnation. To maintain our uniqueness we must retain our zest for challenging and overcoming fear itself."

Sometimes you can feel your emotional drive in the energy you have, perhaps a restlessness, particularly when you are provoked or challenged. It seems to be saying, Let's go, let's go! Some people call this nervous energy, and I believe that worry and insecurity often set it off. I come to this conclusion after interviewing many superachievers, including evangelist Billy Graham, child psychologist Benjamin Spock and Ted Turner.

Turner told me that worry and insecurity drove him to the top of the business and sports worlds. In fact, he said that his father, Ed, seemed to know the secret of business "success" by intentionally raising young Ted to be insecure. After losing his financial fortune during the Depression, advertising salesman Ed sent nine-year-old Ted off to military school. "I was unhappy, but I developed a drive to prove myself, to show that I was a good person," Ted recalls. "In my drive to succeed, I became very organized and planned things for years. My worry seemed to create more energy, and resiliency. And I became proficient under pressure." (But Turner admits his emotional drive became too desperate, too concentrated in work, and his personal life became a shambles.)

"Ordinary" people have also done some incredible things through emotional drive, especially when it is for someone they love. On March 15, 2001, Kenneth Waters walked out of jail in Cambridge, Massachusetts, after being imprisoned for twenty years for murder. He was cleared after his sister, Betty Ann Waters, a former high school dropout, put herself through law school in hopes of someday clearing her brother's name. After graduating, she focused on her brother's case and produced DNA samples which convinced authorities to set him free. "I think it's absolutely incredible that she's dedicated her life to this," he said.

For most of us, our emotional drive and worry system will never become as powerful as Betty Ann Waters' or Ted Turner's. Yet they can become productive for us if we keep perspective. Unfortunately, unhealthy worry seems rampant in our society, causing much distress, even paranoia and illness.

2
Fear's New Focus: The Ego Defense

"If the cave people knew how we were using their adrenaline and endorphins, they'd be surprised."
—Robert S. Eliot, late director of the Institute of Stress Medicine

The Amazing Kreskin is not a macho guy. Admittedly, he's a little nerdy. But he adapts his primitive fear into a powerful force on stage and on television. Billing himself as a practical mentalist who does not dabble in ESP or hocus-pocus, Kreskin sharpens his focus through defense of his ego, which results in nervous energy.

In the 1990s, Kreskin appeared on an internationally-televised show with Robin Leach. He agreed to a segment in which he would try to find his $3,000 paycheck after it was hidden on the set. If he couldn't find it, he wouldn't get paid. "I got nervous. I felt pressure and I was driven, but suddenly my concentration became sharper," he recalled. "It took only ninety seconds, a record for me, and I found the check inside a spice shaker. I don't know how I did it, but somehow I was forced to harness a further aspect of my powers."

Kreskin believes his emergency fear system was triggered by a desire to protect his reputation, his ego. "It was a crisis and it could have hurt my career." My, how some people have trained their ancient fear reaction!

Originally, such a reaction was intended to help us survive physically. As early humans, our job description was pretty straightforward: find regular food and shelter, procreate, and ward off predators and opposing tribes. Nature created fear to motivate us in these areas, especially when our needs were not being met. And to defend against these fears, nature equipped us with survival mechanisms, sometimes known as "defense mechanisms." A classic example of a defense mechanism is the emergency fear system.

As primitive man's brain evolved, he could anticipate possible problems, and thus the worry system developed. Then we started to fashion tools and weapons. There are numerous theories as to why we suddenly got smart. "I would argue that the short answer is fear," says researcher Rush W. Dozier Jr. "Compared to a lion, a tiger or a gazelle, our hominid ancestors were clumsy, unspecialized and weak ... with modern humans, evolution moved away from strength and power as a survival strategy to one that relies almost completely on intelligence and cunning."

Fear in Modern Society

Through superior consciousness, planning, and powers of adaptation, we have gradually overcome (or at least made more manageable) most of the fears that once plagued us. Most of these threats have eventually been overcome because we've acted on our fears. We've arrested AIDS and are closing in on a cancer cure, so why should things like global warming beat us?

In olden days, the threats to our safety were tangible and visible: sabertooth tigers, mastodons, and enemy tribes. Today, our modern civilization and technology, our governments and safety nets, have removed much of the work to satisfy our physical needs. Ironically, we have developed more fears than ever. Through communications we know about things that may be on the way—a recession, company downsizing, crime, or a weather system. We don't live from day to day as much as we used to, and so we acquire fears about days to come.

These new fears—especially irrational fears—can continue to pump unneeded adrenaline and cortisol through our system; hence, the huge problem we have today with distress and anger. Neuroscientist Joseph LeDoux says that fear has taken on pathological consequences in phobias, obsessive-compulsive behavior, panic disorders, anxiety, mental illness, and post traumatic stress disorder—which is another reason to study fear and try to use it productively.

In today's world, the survival game is more psychological and emotional, involving issues of status and society. It's vital that we be somebody. The achievers are the ones who get the trophies, the attention, the power. In a way, it's still survival of the fittest. These days, however, our needs are primarily centered around self-esteem and ego. And out of those needs are born fears—fear of failure, fear of what others think about us and fear of loss of status. Each year, for example, many people die because they refuse to call an ambulance when they have chest pains. They are fearful of bringing the commotion of sirens into their neighborhood. And a late 1990s survey showed that more people were afraid of public speaking than they were of death. One of our biggest fears has become that of embarrassment, of what other people think, of getting our ego bruised. These fears tend to be exaggerated because we have more time to think (and worry) than ever before.

The Link to Our Ancestors

Physically, we still react to fear the same way primitive man did: with our emergency fear system. When we are threatened, our mind alerts the sympathetic nervous system, which alerts the adrenaline system, which sends hormones to enhance our muscles and our senses—the same way it has been doing since human life began. "Physiologically, we are still hunters and gatherers and that will likely be with us for another 150,000 to 200,000 years," says C. Loring Brace, one of the world's leading paleoanthropologists. "All of our basic emotions and capabilities and defensive reactions are shaped by that. But through our learned behavior, we now discourage aggression. The adrenaline and the aggression are still there, but they are not focused." Brace adds, however, that many people do learn to focus these abilities. "It can make us a professional scholar or an entrepreneur or a world-class athlete. (Baseball player) Pete Rose knew how to focus his fight or flight." Perhaps this is also why many of us still seek physical thrills on the ski slopes or through watching a horror movie.

Nevertheless, there are still some practical uses for the caveman's defense. "If we didn't have the ability to be afraid, we'd be walking off cliffs and in front of cars," says Richard Surwit, vice-chair of research of the department of psychiatry and behavioral sciences at Duke University. When faced with a real physical threat, the age-old physical response can have amazing results, especially when it is also triggered by our defense of ego:

- In Bismarck, North Dakota, teenager Stacy Miller rolled her car into a ditch, trapping her friend. Stacy got angry and was suddenly filled with superior strength, pushing the 2,500-pound vehicle off the victim. She was fearful, she said, not only for the safety of her friend, but also because she thought her parents would be angry with her for wrecking the car.
- Eighteen-year-old John Thompson had his arms ripped off by machinery in a farming accident, but staggered 150 feet to his house, twisted door-knobs with his mouth, clenched a pencil in his teeth to phone for help, then waited for paramedics in the bathtub with the curtains wrapped around his body—because he was afraid his mother would get mad at him for getting blood on the floor.

The Ego Defense

In our competitive society, the defense of ego is a driving force behind achievement in many fields. If you tap into it constructively, it can reap rewards, just as it has done for athletes like Doug Flutie. At five feet, nine inches, Flutie should not fit in the National Football League's world of goliaths; and he does not have a strong arm for a quarterback. But his enormous pride makes him seven feet tall. Defense of his ego has not only driven Flutie to develop his skills over the years, it has given him a con-trolled desperation to win game after game. "I love the pressure of the final minutes of a game, of having to prove myself to the critics," he says. As the clock winds down, Flutie says he goes into a type of fight-or-flight mode, using controlled anger to sharpen his concentration. At the most critical moments, he says, the action seems to slow down (in a type of tachypsy-chia), allowing him more time to pick out his receivers or to run through holes in the enemy line. "It's probably something to do with adrenaline; it happens over and over in similar plays."

"Our greatest need is to satisfy our egos," says William J. Beausay, retired president of the Academy of Sports Psychology. "It's the need we all have to feel important. In psychology, we say, 'You never get enough of that wonderful stuff.' That usually means sex, but that's actually No. 2."

For many of us, this ego defense may be subconscious and we may not even know we are employing it. For example, we may be trying extra hard at work not just to get ahead, but to prove to somebody that we can do it. That person may be a parent who was never satisfied, an aloof boss, or ourselves.

The ego defense dominates competitive sports. Carole Seheult, a British sports psychologist and chartered clinical psychologist, has studied how athletes react to situations with psychological and emotional reactions deeply set in their psyche. Seheult and other psychologists refer to these reactions as defense mechanisms, and they can provide extra energy, intensity and determination at crucial times. According to Seheult, "The area of competitive sport, particularly at the elite level, is likely to provide ample opportunity for the exercise of an individual's defense mechanisms. Head-to-head competition or involvement in major championships, where an athlete or player has to be prepared to put himself or herself on the line, to ask of themselves testing questions regarding levels of skill and commitment, and to extend limits of performance, will undoubtedly trigger instinctual feelings of anxiety against which the ego will need to protect itself. Further pressures may also come from external sources such as relationships with coaches, sponsors, officials, and family, as well as internal feelings regarding rivals and opponents."

How will the world perceive us if we lose? It is human nature to ask this question, if only subconsciously—and then it is automatic nature for our fear defense systems to activate with their rushing hormones, increased blood pressure and heart rate. We already know that the mind-body cannot differentiate between threats—whether they are physical or mental, real or perceived, immediate or in the future. Even in a slow activity like golf, the ego defense can raise arousal levels. "When you feel fear about missing a short putt to win a match, the increase in adrenaline, heart rate, blood pressure, and respiration function to prepare your body and mind for action," says Patrick J. Cohn, who works with professional golfers. "Since you're never in physical danger when you play golf, the anxiety you experience is triggered by a perception of threat to your self-esteem or ego."

Besides the two fear defense systems, defense mechanisms include denial, repression, and isolation. They can be positive or negative, adaptive or maladaptive—resulting either in a successful performance or a self-destructive one. For instance, when facing a tough match against a seemingly unbeatable foe, a golfer may react with denial. Successfully used, this denial may help the golfer maintain a high performance level because he is unafraid of the favored opponent and does not accept the danger of the possibility of losing, even when behind on the back nine of a tournament. That is the adaptive reaction. The maladaptive reaction would be for the golfer not to understand the challenge in the skilled opponent and fail to make the required effort to win.

This ego defense can also be seen in areas other than sports. In 1989, I wrote a newspaper article about twin sisters who went on to become a heart surgeon and a clinical psychologist. The interviews went smoothly until I informed the psychologist that, upon second mention of them in the article, I had to refer to her sister as Dr. and to her as Ms. The paper did not recognize psychologists as official doctors. Well, the psychologist became quite irritated and threatened to stop cooperating for the article if she was not referred to as doctor. She was just as successful as her sister, she stressed. They had both scored almost identical, record-shattering academic marks in high school and university. Some people may call this sibling rivalry, but, of course, ego is involved. And what a powerful drive it has.

Without self-consciousness, without ego, there is no competitive sports, no corporate competition. As long as scores are kept, as long as bottom-lines for businesses come into play, ego will be a motivating factor. Competition has become part of our environment, says Alfie Kohn, a lecturer and former teacher, in his book *No Contest: The Case Against Competition*. "We act competitively because we are taught to do so, because everyone else around us does so, because it never occurs to us not to do so, and because success in our culture seems to demand that we do so."

Potential threats to our pride or ego are all around us, or at least nearby:

- Our neighbors' spanking new $50,000 sports utility vehicle, parked twenty feet away from our four-year-old sedan.
- A co-worker's raise or promotion.

- Our relatives' baby, who has learned to talk or walk much sooner than our children.
- Bob's upgraded Internet service, "ten times faster" than ours.
- Your spouse's salary, suddenly more than yours.

While these issues may not run our lives or may not be issues at all if we are totally well-adjusted (are any of us?), they can result in defensive posture, worry, or remedial action.

What People Think

Worrying about what people think, and sometimes acting on that worry, has become endemic in our society, and it produces its own brand of ego defense in specific circumstances.

Even Ned Hallowell (oops, Dr. Ned Hallowell), who has written two insightful books about worry, is sometimes afraid of what others think of him. In the opening chapter of his book *Worry*, he told of a lecture he gave at Cambridge Hospital at Harvard Medical School. Hallowell believes he gave a good talk that day and was congratulated by many people, and yet the face of a woman who apparently did not like the lecture sent the world-renowned psychiatrist crashing to his knees. "Rather than feeling the gentle warmth of a job well done, I felt a chill rising within me," Hallowell recalls. "As my heart pounded, my mind raced to identify the woman and to catalogue all the possible causes of my having upset her. She haunted me for the rest of the day."

Of course, there are many pluses and minuses to worrying about what others think. You can choke under the pressure when people you know are watching. In 2000, Jennifer L. Butler, an assistant professor of psychology at Wittenberg University in Springfield, Ohio, studied the performance of forty-six undergraduate students playing an Atari video game. She discovered that the students got worse scores when people they knew were put into the audience.

The reverse can also be true. In high school, I finished an impressive fifth in an all-Ontario cross-country meet, largely because I ran the entire race next to one of my best friends. I had not trained properly for the race, but my pride would not let me slow down. It must have been my arousal system that got me to the finish line. Even though I didn't consider myself to have a big ego, I didn't want my friend to think less of me, so I rounded up resources I didn't think I had.

At work, you may not need a hugely inflated ego to have your emergency fear system set off from time to time. A simple dose of self-consciousness can get you blushing or your heart palpitating. It may be that you are simply a person who is sensitive, especially to scrutiny or criticism.

3
Understanding Your Fear Reaction

"Amazingly, in almost every situation you face, at least half the battle in alleviating your stress is simply becoming more aware of how you react to situations."
—Jeff Davidson, certified management consultant

Professional golfer Tiger Woods has a secret weapon—fear. During his record-breaking 2000 season, he told me that he often gets scared, and that he acts on that fear. "I get nervous before every shot," he said. "It's how you deal with it that determines whether you will be a success."

Woods understands that even the best golfers generally perform poorly under the increasing pressure of a tournament's final day. (In 2000, despite winning nine tournaments and $9.2 million, his stroke average on Sundays was nearly half a shot worse than in the other three rounds.) "The tension ruins their swing and it makes them old before their time," he said. "I wonder how many of them are aware of it?"

Pressure and Stress

Research shows that most people perform tasks differently under pressure. When your emergency fear system kicks in, your *mind-body chemistry*—the link between thoughts, hormones, and physical responses—changes along with your reactions and your technique. Even if pressure isn't getting to you at work, it may be spilling over to affect you at home.

If you feel pressure (and who doesn't?) what you're really feeling is a type of fear—a type that has a significant impact on most people and their work. We feel pressure to get a job done or to meet a deadline, to keep family and friends happy, to do everything we need to do in the course of a day. We may even feel pressure to live a fulfilled and happy life. Then there's peer pressure, which often convinces us to do things that common sense might tell us to avoid.

Despite countless hours of research, debate, and analysis, we do not yet have a clear understanding of pressure. Like stress, pressure has become an oversimplified cliché, but it's actually a very complicated phenomenon. To label it an ambiguous mystery that can be banished with a few deep breaths is far too convenient.

In order to define pressure—and to separate it from its delinquent cousin, stress—we need to go back to the early 1900s. When building bridges, engineers said that stress was the amount of pressure applied to a bridge by the forces of gravity, earth movement, winds, and weights. It was very important to determine how much stress a bridge would take before it began to crack. In the 1930s, Canadian endocrinologist Hans Selye applied the term *stress* to humans. Selye studied and wrote about the emotional, physical and psychological stresses that affect human beings. Seyle believed, however, that personal stress, unlike the stresses upon a bridge, could be a good thing. Bad (counter-productive) stress became known as *distress* and good (productive) stress became known as *eustress*. According to Seyle, an appropriate amount of stress was good for a person's optimal health and production.

I used to lump stress and pressure together, believing that both were self-imposed. I still think the two are closely related and even act upon one another, but I now believe that pressure is different from stress in that it can sometimes come from an *external* force. Just like the wind and weight on a bridge, pressure can come in the form of a heavy workload, a demanding spouse or an underachieving child. It can also come from the high expectations we have for ourselves. In short, pressure is composed of the demands and expectations placed upon us—either by ourselves or by others.

There are at least three types of pressure:

1. **Physical pressure:** A task, a time deadline, a need to produce income.
2. **Psychological pressure:** Thinking or worrying about something. This may be the most common type of pressure.

3. **Emotional pressure:** Your reaction to a situation or potential situation can cause stress, which can create its own kind of pressure. When you feel stressed, you often get more pressure and more stress, perhaps even frustration.

Stress, on the other hand, comes in the form of mental and physical sensations from within, such as tension or a sick stomach. Stress is our *reaction* to pressure, the result of our emotions being activated. Basically, this is a fear reaction. If we feel pressure to finish a report, for example, our emergency fear system may kick in, producing nervous energy—a common form of stress.

DISTRESS

Everybody feels distress from time to time, usually in the form of tension, loss of concentration, fatigue, nervousness, irritability, or lack of confidence. There are basically two kinds of distress: *acute distress* (our reaction to sudden demands) and *chronic distress* (which makes us feel fearful over a longer time frame).

It is estimated that in the United States, $300 billion a year is lost to stress-related effects such as decreased productivity, increased absenteeism, and employee turnover. Polls suggest that many people feel high levels of distress at work, often making them do things they later regret.

Distress can cause illness. If fears and anxieties remain active for weeks or months, the high levels of cortisol that our emergency fear system releases can become toxic, leaving us more susceptible to colds, flu, backaches, tight chest, migraine headaches, tension headaches, allergy outbreaks, and skin ailments. Chronic stress may have even more serious results: hypertension, ulcers, addictions, asthma, infertility, colon or bowel disorders, diabetes, kidney disease, rheumatoid arthritis, mental illness, heart disease, stroke, cancer, and suicide. Distress can also result in depression, insecurity, poor memory, low energy, and vulnerability to accidents.

DEMANDS

Some experts say that we feel pressure when demands exceed our resources. In other words, if you can usually type 75 words per minute and you have two minutes to type 250 words, you will feel a great deal of pressure, and consequently some distress. When faced with a deadline or competitive situation, people feel varying degrees of pressure and subsequently varying degrees of stress. It is when stress becomes too great and turns to distress that our mental and physical skills break down.

The pressure from demands is increasing in the corporate world, according to James E. Loehr, president and CEO of LGE Performance Systems, which works with companies from investment to banking to cosmetics. "The competitive pressure of everyday life in corporate America today is more intense, demanding and debilitating than ever before," he says. "It's characterized by long hours, frequent travel, a constant need for high levels of concentration, endless competitive pressure, and the ever-present threat of downsizing. We are all expected to accomplish more with less. Companies are being forced to streamline their operations, and streamlining affects everyone involved. We have to learn how to excel in a game that has constantly shifting rules. In today's corporate world, you either perform to the max or you don't play. There's always someone waiting in the wings to jump in and take your place."

The Top 10 Signs That You Are Stressed At Work

10. You have a pain in the neck, stomach, shoulders, back or jaw.
9. You *are* a pain in the neck—to others. Somebody tells you to take a pill.
8. You continually feel a sense of relief.
7. Your concentration or decision-making powers deteriorate.
6. You are in charge of the coffee klatch, or you're always going outside for a smoke.
5. Your desk is littered with empty condiment containers.
4. Your sick days are used up by March.
3. You start talking to your computer—and some days it talks back.
2. You have no energy at home and you don't want to hear about family issues.
1. Your spouse knows the names of all your co-workers.

Perceptions

Some pressures are heavy in their own right: a competition or deadline at work, a mortgage, a car payment or raising children. Other pressures are blown out of proportion, taking on more weight than they deserve. How onerous a particular pressure becomes often depends on our perception. Remember, the emergency fear system and the worry system cannot differentiate between real and imagined threats; they send their hormones rushing to help in both cases.

If many of your pressures are self-imposed, they may be coming from that little voice inside your head—that inner critic who demands high performance (and maybe even perfection). Your inner voice has a way of keeping you insecure, says Helen Graham, a lecturer in psychology at Keele University in England. "It is the way we see and think about the world—our attitude to life—as well as the beliefs we have about it that determines the level of stress we experience," she explains. "We may fear that no one likes us; that we will not succeed at an examination or interview; that we will fail to attract friends and lovers; that we will lose our job or our loved ones; develop painful or debilitating illnesses, and so on. Much of the stress we experience is undoubtedly a product of our imagination, determined by events, circumstances and things that are not externally real. Nevertheless, the stress our imagination produces and the psychological and physical effects of this are very real."

In reality, most pressures *are* threats of a kind. The major problem is that we often see them as being too great to handle. For example, while a deadline does threaten failure to complete a job on time, some of us can't stop there. Some see this possibility as a personal threat to their self-esteem or livelihood. They worry that their boss, their client, or their peers will see them as less of a person if they don't meet the deadline and complete the task.

Identifying Your Fears

Once you have defined what pressure is, you must gauge its presence in your life and work in order to manage it. "You have to pinpoint your stresses [reaction to pressure] at work and then ask yourself to what extent you can remove or at least reduce the impact of that stress," says clinical psychologist Allen Elkin, founder of the Stress Management and Counseling Center in New York. "In some cases, you don't have the ability to eliminate some of the sources of stress: getting the boss transferred may take some doing, and asking for a raise the day after the company announces downsizing plans may not be in your best interest. What you can change, however, is you. You can manage your stress and reduce its consequences."

Exercise: Managing Pressure at Work

Write down the demands that are creating pressure in your job, and determine whether they are affecting your performance. Next, examine the possible internal sources of the pressure you feel:

- Are your own expectations too high or too low?
- Are you dissatisfied with your duties?
- Are you thinking negatively?
- Are you holding on to too much baggage from the past, a feeling of powerlessness, or self-esteem that is too high or too low?

Of course, the primary cause of internally generated pressure—fear—is linked with many of the above factors. It may be fear of failure, fear of not meeting quotas or deadlines, fear of rejection, or fear of job loss or demotion.

Identifying your fears is a crucial part of improving what has become known as your emotional intelligence. "Just as human beings learned to read and to count, so we can become literate about our emotions," says British psychotherapist Frances Wilks. "It requires honesty, learning to name our emotions, feel them fully, reflect on what they're telling us, discover the events that have evoked them. Uncovering fear and working with it may give us the opportunity to transform its energy into useful passion. If we confront what we're feeling, it releases us from being stuck in it."

Don't feel inadequate or weak if you feel fear and pressure at work; research shows that almost everybody does. At the University of Southern California, researcher Robert Karasek and his colleagues discovered that the two most stressful aspects of a job are pressure to perform (tight deadlines, limited resources, productions quotas, severe consequences for failing to meet management's goals) and a lack of control over the work process.

According to psychology professor Robert E. Thayer, high levels of tension are easy to recognize, but moderate levels or slight declines in our energy reserves are not. He adds that most people have little experience in identifying tension, nervousness or anxiety. Furthermore, the cause of tension and distress—fear—is generally misunderstood and stigmatized by society. "Many young boys are taught that fear is unmasculine, so the feeling of tension is ignored," Thayer says. "Only sissies succumb to pressure, or so they are taught."

Sometimes you don't even need a solid reason to feel pressure. It can be caused by lack of focus and letting your mind wander into negative thinking, a common human trait. "Have you ever noticed how uptight you feel when you're caught up in your thinking?" says Richard Carlson, author of *Don't Sweat the Small Stuff*.

Exercise: Identifying Your Pressure Points

To help discover your internally generated pressures, it's useful to identify your attitudes toward work, your goals, and others. Some healthy fears may lead to production, but unhealthy fears can cause unnecessary pressure. Consider the following questions.

- How do you feel when somebody else wins a promotion, a raise, or employee of the month? (It's probably healthy to feel a bit envious, but are you really jealous?)
- How do you feel if you win?
- What are your goals? How closely are they related to your ego or pride?
- How do you respond to criticism? Are you taking things too personally?

If you answered the questions honestly, you'll now have a better understanding of your personal pressure points. The next step is to understand how that pressure is affecting your performance.

The Impact of Fear and Pressure on Performance

Generally, pressure seems to impair skill, focus, and confidence but improve effort, says Roy Baumeister, a professor of psychology at Case Western University. Baumeister studied World Series baseball games between 1924 and 1982, and discovered that when seventh and deciding games were needed, the home teams won only 40.8 percent of the time, thanks partly to an increase in errors. Baumeister believes that the home teams felt more pressure to win in front of their fans and were thus more self-conscious (i.e., more afraid). Similarly, a study of the British Open golf championship revealed that the scores of contending British players deteriorated more than those of contending foreign players from the first to the final round. When it comes to physical tasks, research shows that a slight increase in heart rate in response to fear can improve performance, but additional stress can cause a rapid deterioration, especially in tasks involving fine motor skills.

The impact of the emergency fear response on non-physical tasks is more subtle and harder to establish. For example, the success of a Wall Street trader who pockets millions in a single session may be attributed to experience, organization, risk-taking and use of contacts—and yet all of these factors can be enhanced with the optimal amount of fear.

"Many companies don't realize a good dose of fear of losing helps sharpen survival instincts," says CEO Andrew Grove, who has forged Intel into a profitable Fortune 500 company.

My research substantiates that fear and insecurities may be the biggest motivators in human history—the driving forces in sports and entertainment, big business and in the building of entire civilizations. High rollers such as Bill Gates, Bill Clinton, Monica Seles, Ted Turner, and Michael Jordan have learned the secrets of fear management. They know that fear is crucial to peak performance because it creates pressure and hormonal fuels that act as an additive to skill.

How the Emergency Fear System Affects Skills

(The average heart rate is 70 beats per minute.)

Fine motor skills (hand dexterity, hand-eye coordination, writing a report, driving a car): You can perform well at low to medium levels of arousal, up to 115 heartbeats per minute, but then the dexterity of the fingers is lessened.

Complex motor skills (involving a series of muscle groups and movements requiring hand-eye coordination, precision, tracking and timing): These skills begin to deteriorate at about 145 heartbeats per minute.

Gross motor skills (involving the large muscle groups and strength and speed activities such as running, fighting): These skills actually improve as the level of arousal rises.

In elite sports, fear-driven pressure has produced some great performances (see Chapter 14). "It took me some time to realize it, but I love pressure," says

Michael Johnson, the only man to win Olympic gold medals in both the 200- and 400-meter races. "I know that sounds nuts because we've been trained to think of pressure as the enemy, the unfair burden that holds us down."

In entertainment, performers such as comedian Jackie Gleason, actress Marilyn Monroe, and singer Ricky Martin have used their nervousness to sharpen their acts. "Fear and insecurity are what my show is all about; they're what the whole world is about," says TV talk show host Oprah Winfrey. "Deep down, I've never felt good about myself and this is what has driven me. My fears and insecurities never let me rest."

But, most people are held down by pressure, says John R. Noe, mountain climber, author and president of IMH Systems. "Far too many people go to their graves with songs that were never written, pictures that were never painted, businesses that were never built, troubled hearts that were never gladdened," he says. "The reason? Fear."

Exercise: Identifying Your Fear Reaction

If you want to improve your performance under pressure—whether you're an athlete, a secretary, a scholar, or a factory worker—you must become aware of your personal reaction to pressure and fear. Ask yourself the following questions:

- Do I feel too much pressure or tension?
- Where does it come from?
- Am I aware that my fear systems contribute to both pressure and how I react to it?
- Generally, do I perform better under pressure, or worse?

If you can answer these questions, you are well on your way to good performance. We all like to think that we know ourselves, but there may be things about your own pressures and the way you cope with them of which you are not fully aware.

Test yourself over the next few weeks. Is pressure causing you frustration or depression, leaving you wound up like a cheap watch? Does it give you an adrenaline buzz or a feeling of control? Do you respond by channeling the fear energy into your task, or does it result in sloppy work and missed deadlines? Are your pressure levels too low, leaving you bored?

II
Management

In this section, we will discuss ways to keep pressure at a manageable level so that we are not continually suffering from tension or the jitters. In Chapter 4, we see that using your resources can stabilize you at work. Chapter 5 focuses on your ability to change your emotions when they are hindering you. Chapter 6 shows the best level for arousal in a job lasting at least several hours. In Chapter 7, we see that everyone reacts to pressure in a different way, and that personal techniques may be needed.

4
Resources to the Rescue

"Stress management is when you take action after it becomes a problem. Pressure management is learning to manage the pressures in your life and your responses to them, so that you are less likely to reach the point of stress."
—Gael Lindenfield and Malcolm Vandenburg, authors of *Positive Under Pressure*

Every year, when lists of the most stressful jobs are published, the president of the United States is at or near the top. If this is a stressful job, the presidents sure aren't showing it. In fact, we ought to study how they handle pressure. They would probably teach us that we have more control over pressure, fear, and stress than we think.

Historians tell us that presidents often perform exceptionally with the weight of the world on their shoulders, usually maintaining good mental and physical health. They hold up—even thrive—under pressure, thanks to several key strategies. They delegate many jobs to their advisors. They eat right, exercise often, and use entertainment, sports, and humor as escapes from reality. After his first day in the Oval Office, George W. Bush sat back and watched *Stupid Behavior Caught on Tape*, which featured a prisoner getting his head stuck in the bars of his cell, pallbearers dropping a coffin, and a farmer wrecking his own tractor. A friend said he chortled at the show. Many presidents have also been music lovers. Bill Clinton played the saxophone, Harry Truman entertained servicemen on the piano, and Richard Nixon was more serious on the keyboard with his love for classical music.

Our jobs may not carry the weight of the world, but we can use similar strategies to keep our work pressure at manageable levels. In fact, you already possess the necessary tools—your job skills, your patience and discipline, your support network of colleagues, and even your attitude and genetic makeup.

Physical Resources

Good health and abundant energy can be powerful resources—resources that you can control by eating a balanced diet, exercising, and getting the proper amount of sleep. But don't be discouraged if you succumb to pressure on some days and not others, or at some times of the day and not others. Our emergency fear system tends to be more vulnerable when our energy is down or when we are tired.

Many companies provide a gymnasium, yoga classes, or exercise classes. If yours does not, make it a routine to walk around and stretch several times during the course of each day. Even rocking on a chair has been shown to relieve tension. Some people keep chewing gum or Vitamin C tablets in their desk drawer. A stress-buster, such as a rubber ball that you can squeeze when you get tense, a cuddly animal, or a picture of your family can help take the edge off your stress.

Of course, the most practical physical resources you have at work are your job skills. If you are competent at what you do, you will have more confidence and less fear. And confidence is vital in managing pressure. With a changing workforce, you may need to upgrade your skills periodically. Learning more about the goals and objectives of your company and your department can also help.

An often neglected resource is the people around us—our colleagues or bosses. We can ease much of our pressure through their support, advice, companionship, and contributions, or by delegating an overload of work. A feeling of "being in it together" can significantly reduce pressure on any one individual.

If your pressures are largely external, you may have more control than you think. You can improve your posture, lighting, and seating, and reduce neck and eye tension by putting your computer screen at eye level (try propping it up with old phone books). You can wind down by forcing yourself to take breaks. If someone else controls these issues, talk to your human resources department about improving the situation. What about listening to music while you work—perhaps on headphones?

It's also worth noting that hot temperatures can raise tension levels. Pierce J. Howard, director of research for the Center for Applied Cognitive Studies in Charlotte, North Carolina, advises employers to make special provisions for those who work in temperatures of more than 90° Fahrenheit.

Exercise: Managing External Pressures

- Do the dirty work you hate as soon as possible. It increases your discipline and patience and gives you incentive because you know that more enjoyable tasks are ahead.
- Organize your desk.
- Schedule your day and week, but don't set unrealistic deadlines.
- Learn to say no if you are overtaxed; Superman is a fictional character.
- Make yourself a team player, helping others or encouraging team projects.
- Delegate, or train others.
- Take enough breaks.
- Slow down and relax when possible.
- Listen to music (if you have access to it).
- Eat a balanced diet and eat lunch out of the office.
- Get enough exercise and enough sleep.
- Take all of your vacation time.

Mental Resources

Although some external pressures may be beyond your reach, most internal pressures are not, says psychologist Steve Randall. "I believe that the pressure we feel is largely under our control. Rather than being built into certain jobs, most pressure seems to be added to neutral situations because of our attitude, perspective, or confusion about values and goals."

Perspective may be our greatest resource. If you can put your job into perspective, it should ease your pressure and perhaps put your hormones at an optimal level, where they can be a boost rather than a burden. "The perception of threat, real or imagined, immediately triggers the release of (sometimes toxic) chemicals of distress," says corporate and athletic stress coach James E. Loehr. "Change perception and the chemistry changes. Change your perception of your DI, boss or coworker from a maddening psycho to a positive toughening force and the distress goes away."

Michael Crawford of Nepean, Ontario, is a sales account manager for Nortel. He often sees business people blowing a job out of proportion and causing themselves distress. "I tell them that it is not a life-and-death situation, that I've been in a life-and-death situation and I know the difference," he says. In 1996, Crawford pulled a drowning friend from the Rideau Canal. The accident had a profound affect on Crawford, a go-getting, self-proclaimed Type A personality who is very successful at his job. After the accident, Crawford realized that too much work was stressing him out. He went to a psychologist and now puts his work into perspective, balancing it with chores around his house, chopping wood, and rebuilding old cars.

Richard Carlson, stress consultant and author of *Don't Sweat the Small Stuff*, agrees with Crawford's analysis. "I've had hundreds of clients over the years who have all but neglected their families as well as their own dreams because of their propensity to believe that life is an emergency. They justify their neurotic behavior by believing that if they don't work eighty hours a week, they won't get everything done. Sometimes I remind them that when they die, their in basket won't be empty!"

Once we start taking responsibility for the pressures and subsequent stresses that affect us, they will drop to manageable levels, according to authors Gael Lindenfield and Malcolm Vandenburg: "Once you stop blaming outside forces and take full responsibility for your own feelings, you are able to begin to alter them, without having to worry about the external triggering factors. You are able to relax while your colleagues pull their hair out, your children continue to misbehave, your partner stays in exile, and the traffic continues to roar past your house."

It's also important to realize that pressure is not necessarily a bad thing. Think about an important bridge match, a wedding, a romantic date, a party. Each of these events carries some pressure, but they can also be fun. It is your perception that will determine the outcome. If you look upon the pressure as nerve-wracking stress, you probably won't enjoy the event or succeed; if you think of it as excitement, however, you will flourish.

Years ago, at my wedding party, we had a sing-along with a microphone. A relative who was a good singer kept approaching the mike throughout the evening, but he let his fear of singing in front of others prevent him from ever getting there—but I know he would have had an enriching time if he could have just gotten over it. I force myself to remember that incident whenever I tend to seize up about doing something I know I would enjoy. That happened in 1998 when the British Broadcasting Company invited me to come to New York to take part in a documentary. Nervous, I found myself thinking up excuses as to why I could not attend. Then, I remembered that unfulfilled relative. I flew to Manhattan and enjoyed the taping. I believe I did a good job because I didn't let the pressure overwhelm me. I let it work for me. Deep down, I guess I knew I had the resources to get me through it.

In these unsettled times, adaptability and creativity are valuable in keeping pressures down. Positive thinking is another key resource, but it may not be as important as dumping negative thinking. "Most of us are still carrying distressful experiences that everyone else involved has forgotten about," says Leslie Bendaly, a Toronto consultant and author of *Winner Instinct*. "But we just can't let go. And that weight, in a small or large way, limits our abilities. Sometimes burdens become familiar companions and we hesitate to release them. Those who have learned to walk fast on thin ice identify their burdens and they get rid of them. They make sure they are traveling light."

On a deeper scale, our beliefs and attitudes about the world and ourselves can also cause pressure. If you suffer from low self-esteem and believe that others are superior, you will probably fear more things at work. If you feel good about yourself, generally you will fear less. Self-esteem is a valuable resource in the demands-versus-resources game of pressure.

Exercise: Managing Internal Pressures

- Phone someone who's positive, just to talk.
- Set goals for yourself and write them down, but keep expectations realistic.
- Consider the perspective of your boss.
- Change your routine, even if just slightly.
- Let go sometimes; have a dress-down day once in a while.
- Keep a sense of humor.
- If your inner critic is too much of a perfectionist, tell it to please be quiet.
- Keep your job in perspective.
- Leave your work at work, and live a balanced life.
- Remind yourself that you are valuable, a good person.

Emotional Resources

Emotions can be powerful resources, but they can also add to pressure and derail our performance. Anger, for one, can mobilize our fear and give us added energy and focus, but it can also lead to frustration and wayward energy. We have to learn to manage our emotions.

One of the key emotional resources is an ability to detach yourself from a situation—particularly if you are in charge. "Perhaps the most valuable quality of a senior executive is his or her ability to function in a crisis," says business consultant and lecturer Brian Tracy. "This ability is solely a result of refusing to get caught up in the emotionality of the moment."

Just knowing that you have resources at hand can give you confidence, which some people consider to be an emotion. While writing this book there were times that I felt drained and strained, but reminding myself that I had determination, skill and a wide network of experts to help me was enough to get me back on track.

Nothing balances pressures and reduces tension like spirituality—a reflective, less self-conscious, more well-rounded way of life. Some people put so much emphasis on their work that it becomes a central part of their identity. When introduced to someone, they immediately begin to talk about their work rather than other valuable areas of life, such as family, friends, or involvement in the community.

CNN founder Ted Turner encourages people to examine the amount of time and effort they put into their jobs. "At one time, I didn't realize how much pressure I was putting on myself to achieve, to always be the best," he said. "It became a manic, unhealthy drive to reach the pinnacle and I don't think it made me happy. I didn't have much time for my five children or my personal life." Turner tried to unwind through competitive sailboat racing. He captained the United States to the America's Cup yacht championship in 1977, bringing the same intensity and desire to be Number One onto the waters. "If we were losing, I'd want to jump out of the boat and push," he recalled. Now, Turner has found more relaxing ways of escaping and relieving some of his work pressures, through relaxing with his family and non-competitive hobbies like fishing.

Developing your spirituality can reduce self-consciousness and the influence of ego. "So often we are immobilized by the slightest criticism," says

Richard Carlson. "We treat it like an emergency and defend ourselves as if we were in a battle." He suggests that we occasionally agree with criticism, either to defuse a situation or to learn something about ourselves.

"Learn to stand back and evaluate the opinions of others unemotionally," says Brian Tracy. "It's not easy, but it saves a lot of wear and tear on your system."

Management consultant Jeff Davidson recommends that people compete with themselves and not others. "You don't want to engage in unhealthy, workaholic efforts that deplete your mental, physical, and emotional energy," he says. "Instead, you should seek to lessen your focus on what others are doing and increase your focus on how to be the best you can be."

Although it can be argued that competition drives excellence, competition is not always necessary to thrive, Davidson says. "Examples abound of people who chose to carve their own path with little or no concern for the competition. Michael Dell in PC manufacturing, Jeff Bezos [Amazon.com] in online bookselling, Charles Schwab in the brokerage business, and Fred Smith [Federal Express] in overnight express services are among the many career achievers who not only paid little heed to what the competition was doing, they carved out new territory for themselves."

Exercise: Admit to Choking

Here is one way to relieve an overdose of pressure: admit that you have choked from time to time. Everybody chokes, including the best in every field: Donald Trump, Bill Gates, Madonna, George Bush, and Karrie Webb. Say it out loud: "I have choked." There, doesn't that make you feel better? But just because you occasionally freeze under duress does not mean that you are a *choker* (just as a person who drinks occasionally should not be considered a drinker). And so, here is another out-loud proclamation to practice: "I am not a choker."

5
Changing Your Emotions

"... these are hormones which tend to keep going in the direction you send them."
—Prof. Redford Williams, Duke University

Martin "Buzzy" Schwartz was starting to panic on the floor of the American Stock Exchange. The market had dropped and he was staring a big financial loss in the face. Suddenly, Schwartz grabbed a brown paper bag, put it over his head and started jumping from desk to desk like a wild man, screaming: "I'm long! I'm long! I'm f———long!" (a broker's term, without the profanity). His stunned colleagues burst into laughter. The tension receded from Buzzy's shoulders and he became calm, a clear thinker once more. He returned to his desk and was soon ahead $100,000.

In the next two chapters, we will look at how to transform our mind-body chemistry to our advantage, as Buzzy Schwartz did. For work purposes, we can do this on three different levels: by modifying our moods prior to an important job, by maintaining an optimal level of arousal on the day of the job, and by occasionally switching gears when we become too nervous (to be discussed in Section III). First, let's look at moods.

Moods: Mixing the Right Stuff

Moods are not exactly the same as emotions, but they share similarities and certainly have an effect on our emotional state (and vice versa). Moods are usually less intense and longer lasting than emotions, but they can be more powerful. Everything we do in the course of a day, especially during a pressure event, is filtered through our mood. Moods are complex states, usually determined through the interaction of biorhythms, diet, exercise, sleep, atmosphere, stress level, and drugs. If stress can contribute to our mood, the reverse is also true. If you are in a negative mood, for example, your emergency fear system may kick in more often than it would if your mood were different.

Moods help establish your frame of mind prior to a task. They can also affect your worry system and make you fret about unnecessary things. Mood expert Robert E. Thayer goes further: "In many ways, moods are at the core of our being. A good mood can help us carry out a disagreeable task—it has a way of improving our outlook. Even an unpleasant social interaction can be tolerable if our mood is positive. If we are in a bad mood, an activity that usually is pleasant and gives us enjoyment can be boring and uninteresting."

Moods can be all over the place, but according to stress researcher Pierce J. Howard, they are highly susceptible to personal control and at times can be changed quite easily. People using a strategy of *active mood management* combine relaxation, stress management, thought processes, and exercise. This strategy encompasses a wide range of mind-body systems, including the emergency fear system. "Our bodies do not operate as a series of independent systems," says Thayer. "Instead, moods follow general patterns and affect the entire body. If one element in the system is modified, other elements change, as well. Reducing muscle tension also alters tension-related thoughts, and vice versa."

When I lived in Calgary, I used this method while playing noon-hour basketball games at the YMCA. Not only was the exercise good, so was the social contact. And because I believed that both would improve my mood, I went into the activity with a positive frame of mind, which I am sure added to the good mix. When I went back to work, I usually felt more relaxed and energized.

Some people have their own ways of improving mood, such as personal relaxation techniques, hobbies, or playing with a pet. Some people use power naps in the middle of the day, including former U.S. president Bill Clinton, who often got by on four to six hours a night, but took naps of five to thirty minutes each day (sometimes while leaning against a wall). This type of *passive mood management* involves a measure of escape; watching television is the most popular method.

The most immediate method of influencing moods and emotions is to use the power of your own thoughts. Simple thoughts can rapidly change our emotional chemistry through the limbic system in the center of the brain, sometimes referred to as the emotional brain. When the system receives a signal (a thought), the emotional response time can be as little as twelve one-thousandths of a second. In the blink of an eyelash our emotion can change from fear to anger, or from anger to joy. These neural messages motivate physiological changes as powerful hormones are released throughout the mind-body.

In order to understand this process, recall how your emotions and physical sensations can fluctuate wildly when you go to the movies. You can be scared to death one moment, laughing uncontrollably the next, and crying on your way out. And all through the fantasy of pictures! In fact, James E. Loehr compares the power of our thoughts to Hollywood. He calls the summoning of emotions on command "acting," and he's been teaching it for years to the world's elite athletes and corporate warriors. "The ON switch for an emotion can be fully activated regardless of whether it fits reality as judged by the rational brain," he says. "And once the switch is pulled and the emotion takes

Exercise: The Power of Positive Thinking

To show you how simple thoughts can change your emotions and your chemistry, think for a while about these scenarios:

1. Your boss or relative has criticized you unfairly.
2. You have just discovered you have a serious illness.

Let these thoughts take shape. Don't you feel irritated, physically and mentally? Nothing has really happened, you have just been pondering the possibilities. Now, let's consider some better thoughts:

1. You've just won a million bucks in the lottery.
2. The most beautiful person in the room is flirting with you.

How do you feel now? On top of the world?

Now, let's reverse the first two scenarios. Try thinking that your boss or relative was criticizing you because he was having a bad day. Whew, it wasn't about you after all. A sigh of relief and warmer physical chemistry sweeps through you. And now you discover that the serious illness you had was wrongly diagnosed by your quack doctor. You're OK! Wow, doesn't relief feel good?

Let's keep going. Uh-oh, you really didn't win the lottery. It was a typographical error on your ticket. And you know that gorgeous one—he or she was using you to make someone else jealous. Disappointed? A little depressed?

This exercise proves that our mind-body can react to simple thoughts or fantasies in much the same way as it responds to actual events. Many psychologists and bio-chemists believe the nervous system can't tell the difference between real and perceived threats or joys. In both cases, the adrenaline and the endorphins start flowing. So, through simple thought, you can write yourself a prescription for the internal drugs you want.

---

hold, the feelings we experience simply confirm that the underlying physio-logical mechanisms have been activated. What we feel when we are nervous, anxious, angry, or joyous are the mental and physical consequences of highly specific hormonal surges."

The Alliance of Emotions

If negative thoughts or moods are affecting your performance, or if your con-centration is frazzled, it may mean that you are caught in the emotion of fear. You need a change of chemistry. A healthy dose of fear can be a good thing, but in large amounts it pumps too much adrenaline and cortisol into your sys-tem. The result? You freeze, your skills "choke" or you flee like a rabbit. You need to get out of the fear mode and into a more proactive frame of mind.

To turn fear into a proactive force, we need to make it an ally. We can do this by enveloping it in an emotion that is less threatening to us—such as excitement, joy or even anger. These are feelings that motivate us and get us moving forward, both mentally and physiologically. I call this process the *alliance of emotions*.

The emotion you choose to ally with fear will depend upon the situation. You may want to experiment and eventually narrow your focus through trial and error. See what works best for you. It may be humor, joy, or thoughts of a loved one. If you have problems making the transition from fear to the more passionate emotion, you might need a cue word or phrase (such as "Now!" or "Yes!" or "Action!") to shake the fear loose. Actors and athletes use this method all the time. If you choose to try it, make your cue word a personal thing. It should be something strong that will snap you out of the freeze mode and into a proactive state of mind. The following are some emotions you might want to use in combination with fear. You may want to experiment with each of them at various times and decide which works best for you in particular situations.

Intelligent Anger

Anger is a powerful emotion that can get your fear moving. According to clinical psychologist David W. Edgerly, "Anger tends to emerge when people experience fear, hurt, or intense frustration and in the face of these emotions, humans are designed to become mobilized for action." Controlled anger can mobilize fear, according to Redford Williams, a professor of psychiatry and psychology at Duke University. Anger gets fear moving forward by introducing noradrenaline and dopamine into the emergency reaction, he says, "and these are

Anger at Work

Golfer Nancy Lopez used anger to win an LPGA championship after she felt she'd been unfairly penalized for slow play. "I made anger work to my advantage. I went into tunnel vision. I didn't see the galleries, the TV cameras. I was going to show the LPGA and its officials that I could win in spite of them all. I promise you, nobody could have beaten me that day. I got into a zone where I could see every shot before I hit it, and every shot was perfect in my mind. It was a matter of pride."

- **Thoughts:** A competitor taking your rewards away. A time you felt you were wronged. Your son's unkempt bedroom.
- **Mindset:** Dammit, I will not give in. I'll show them; I refuse to let my colleagues or myself down. I can't let this chance for extra power and control get away.
- **Cue words:** Dammit! I'll show you! Attack!
- **Hormones triggered:** Noradrenaline, dopamine, testosterone (especially through thoughts of dominance), cortisol and some adrenaline.

hormones which tend to keep going in the direction you send them. If you begin to think in a confident, aggressive way, they will help you to continue in that mindset and that physiology."

But be careful once the fear is transformed into anger. According to Los Angeles psychiatrist Mark Goulston, fear can take control of you. "The key is to turn anger into focus and determination."

You don't really have to be angry; you can fake it. If you are stuck in the emotion of fear—perhaps worried that you will lose to a competitor—you can alter your chemistry and mindset by become angry (only in your head) at a colleague or competitor for taking away some of your business. If you can't find somebody else to get mad at, try getting angry with yourself: "This is the last time I'm letting myself down."

Don't let this attitude last for too long, or it will change your mood from afraid to aggressive for the rest of the day. Anger is best used as a short bridge away from fear. After as little as a minute of anger, you may be free of your fear and in a more constructive mood. Let go of the anger and carry on with your work. "You are perhaps most powerful and best prepared when you are angry," says clinical psychologist Neil Clark Warren, founder of Associated Psychological Services in Pasadena, California. "That's why anger is dangerous; mishandling all that power can create havoc and distress. Once you are angry, the challenge is to make rapid and effective use of the anger energy."

EXCITEMENT

If you are uncomfortable with anger, a general feeling of excitement or passion can also mobil-

---

Excitement at Work

Calgary bingo player Muriel Thomas has learned to play up to thirty cards simultaneously in each game. Whenever she gets nervous and starts fumbling, she whispers "Gonna Win! Gonna Win! Gonna Win!" with each number she covers on her cards, and her concentration and confidence both improve.

- **Thoughts:** A part of your job that you enjoy or gain satisfaction from. What you will do tonight when you get home from work.
- **Mindset:** I am looking forward to the challenge of this job. I am going to be satisfied or rewarded. I will not be denied or beaten by fear. Success is a split-second away!
- **Cue words:** Yes! Now! Challenge!
- **Hormones triggered:** Dopamine, noradrenaline, some adrenaline.

ize your fear. Members of the Australian pop group Girl Thing "get a little bit nervous about a gig," according to singer Nikki Stuart. "But we look on it as getting excited rather than nervous. That helps us perform better." Passion and excitement are broad emotions, but they can be a good starting point for a transition away from fear. You're not afraid of a meeting with the boss, you tell yourself; you are excited by the prospect of learning something, of growing, or of having an opportunity to impress her.

LOVE

"I won't be scared for long, not when I think about this powerful love," wrote singer-songwriter David Sereda for his lover. If anything can transform fear, it is the emotion of love, whether it's romantic or platonic. Thinking of others makes us less self-conscious, taking the focus away from our own fear.

Nature seems to know this. I have interviewed hundreds of victims of accidents and assaults who said that they had so-called life flashbacks that motivated them to get through the situation. Michael Persinger, a neuro-

> ### Love at Work
>
> Chris Geel, an amputee, was struggling alone in the northern California desert for four days following an accident. Near death, he thought of his wife and two daughters. He felt a sudden surge of power and dragged himself to the road for help.
>
> - **Thoughts:** Your spouse, your children or your company needing you.
> - **Mindset:** I will not let my family down.
> - **Cue words:** Jennifer! On Wisconsin! My family loves me.
> - **Hormones triggered:** DHEA, serotonin, oxytocin.

scientist at Laurentian University in Sudbury, Ontario, says that just thinking of a loved one during a time of tension or crisis can change a person's emotional chemistry—either spurring their emergency fear system to great accomplishments or soothing their anxiety.

In less threatening circumstances, such as a job interview, imagining a loved one can fill us with warm feelings. As the hormones serotonin and DHEA are released into our system, we gain perspective and confidence. If thoughts alone don't do the trick, a simple prop can also help. When approaching a pressure-filled day, wear something reflective of a loved one and look at it or touch it when you become nervous.

HUMOR

Humor can be the best antidote for tension and the best ally of fear. When you laugh, the hormone endorphin—a painkiller much more potent than morphine—is released through your system. Laughing also lowers blood pressure, forces you to breathe deeply, reduces distress hormones, relaxes your muscles, boosts immune functions, and generally induces a feeling of happiness.

We need to make a conscious effort to incorporate humor into our working lives. Too many workplaces are overly serious. In fact, adults in general are too serious. On average, a child laughs 400 times a day, an adult only 15. "We all start life with a sense of humor, but it gets knocked out of us," says Lila Green, who gives seminars on humor to companies and associations. "The messages we get are 'Wipe that smile off your face,' or 'Act your age' or 'Don't laugh in church.' And we separate learning and work and play too much."

Workplaces need to lighten things up, says C.W. Metcalf, an author who provides humor programs for businesses and hospitals. "If you can't promise people job security—and you can't any more—then you better promise them the most positive, enjoyable work environment they can have."

Humor at Work

U.S. President Ronald Reagan, just after being shot in an assassination attempt, eased everyone's fears, including his own, by telling his wife, "Honey, I forgot to duck."

- **Thoughts:** If my boss is so threatening, why does he have a mustard stain on his shirt?
- **Mindset:** I will survive. No situation is above laughter. Trouble, I laugh in your face because I know I have fear as my ally.
- **Cue words:** Hah!
- **Hormones triggered:** Endorphins, serotonin, even dopamine and noradrenaline in certain instances.

CONFIDENCE

While most people don't see confidence as an emotion, I believe it can be. Many people consider confidence to be a frame of mind that comes and goes depending on circumstances or the weather. We don't give confidence enough credit because it is not as clearly defined as emotions such as anger, joy, and grief. Confidence is the opposite of freezing in the fear reaction. I believe that confidence is related to other emotions and gets the adrenaline, dopamine, and endorphins going in the right direction. If confidence is not a full-blown emotion, it is at least a valuable link between emotion and reason. In pressure situations, confidence is vital—it allows you to trust your skills.

Confidence at Work

After several years of working in small diners, Houston waiter John Cannata was so nervous about his first day at an exclusive restaurant he could hardly get his jacket on. But during a telephone conversation, his girlfriend reminded him of his past successes and of how much customers had liked him. A feeling of poise enveloped him and he went on to a successful debut (and a record number of tips).

- **Thoughts:** Past successes and accolades.
- **Mindset:** I have competent resources and most of the time they will bring me success.
- **Cue words:** You the man! Just show up!
- **Hormones triggered:** Adrenaline, noradrenaline, dopamine, some endorphins and serotonin.

6

The Best Level of Arousal

"You have up to three seconds, between the time an episode occurs and your (emergency fear system) begins to rev up, to exert control."
—clinical research psychologist Steven L. Fahrion

In the previous chapter, we talked about how to manage our emotions and mobilize our feelings of fear prior to suitably responding to a pressure situation. Now let's get down to the task itself. If the situation is a difficult one, if there are considerable demands on us, we will likely feel pressure and some fear arousal as our mind-body goes through chemical changes. We need to find the most comfortable and efficient level of arousal for the job. This is generally known as the *optimal level of arousal*. When you are at your optimal level, you are humming along and your resources are working at pretty close to maximum efficiency. We can probably all recall times like that. We might not have been aware that there was an underlying emergency fear response in our emotional state and we probably didn't care. All that mattered is that we were working effectively.

If you can remain at an optimal level of arousal, you are in control of your hormones. If you cannot, these same hormones may end up controlling you. Under pressure, there is more of a chance that your nervousness will put you above optimal arousal rather than below it. In order to remain "in the zone," we often need to reduce the arousal.

Generally, optimal arousal is preferred over heightened arousal. While heightened arousal can be effective over the short term—especially in sports, physical jobs, and confrontations—jobs that take hours to complete require relative calm and relaxation. You cannot afford to be too psyched up.

Every person has his or her own optimal level of arousal for a particular task. On an arousal scale of one to five, for example, at level two I may be able to type an important report to deadline. But because of your advanced metabolism, skill and confidence, you may be able to handle an arousal level of one. Or maybe you're a beginner, and level one is your best bet.

Different tasks may also require different levels of arousal. If I am running in a race, my arousal level can be fairly high (up to four on the scale) because the emergency fear system is well-suited to such explosion events. On the other hand, if I am drawing a sketch by computer to a deadline, the perfect arousal level would be lower, since arousal tends to be detrimental to fine motor skills.

In general, we should search for a state of mind and chemistry that will last for hours. Robert Thayer says that for most people, a mental and emotional state he calls *calm energy* is ideal for many mental chores. During periods of calm energy, your heart rate, metabolism, and respiration rates are relatively high and you are focused fully on your task, but you feel no urgency, just a quiet and relaxed attention. If you were pressed about it, you might say you were feeling energetic and confident. Thayer also identifies states that are not as conducive to good work: *calm tiredness*, *tense energy*, and *tense tiredness*.

Exercise: Finding Calm Energy

Each of us needs to find calm energy—our personal optimal level of arousal—for the tasks we are to perform. Once again, personal awareness is the first step. When you are in pressure situations, you must identify your arousal levels. Ask yourself the following questions:

- Am I getting so jittery at important meetings that I make too many mistakes or fear speaking up?
- Is my work suffering because I am too pumped?

If you answered yes, you may be getting too aroused. You either need to lower your arousal level or lower the pressure you are under. On the other hand, if you find yourself bored or uninterested, you may have to raise your arousal level and become more alert and motivated.

Clinical psychologist Henry Svec recommends that you monitor the outcome of jobs in relation to your emotional arousal, perhaps in a log or diary. "It is necessary to continue to self-analyze the appropriateness of the emotional arousal levels and successful completion of the task. By doing this, we begin to develop a personalized emotional-performance profile which will guide us in performing to our potential at all times."

Optimal Arousal Levels

Arousal Level		Situation in Which This Level Is Optimal
high arousal		
↑		
extremely excited	5	Life-or-death situations
somewhat excited	4	Explosion sports (football, sprinting), heavy lifting
aroused but not excited	3	Acting, singing, public speaking (at least to start the session)
somewhat aroused	2	Bowling, typing to a deadline, giving a presentation
slightly aroused	1	Painting a picture, writing a detailed report
low arousal		

Coming Down from High Arousal

When you find yourself outside a state of calm energy, what you are feeling is a type of fear reaction. Your emergency fear system has been activated and it wants to follow its natural course—a physical response or a release. Since you are not about to get into a wrestling match with anyone in the office, you can do one of two things: relax back into your optimal level of arousal or, in special, short-term situations, channel the emotions into your work (as will be discussed in Section III). In other words, we can use or defuse the fear. There are many techniques at your disposal—including the use of music, cue words, or visualization (imagining what you want to accomplish).

If anger and frustration are your problems, you must establish control within a matter of seconds; otherwise these emotions can overpower you, says clinical research psychologist Steven L. Fahrion: "You have to avoid [uncontrolled] anger. You have up to three seconds, between the time an episode occurs and your [emergency fear system] begins to rev up, to exert control."

Each of the stress-controlling techniques described in the following pages has the same objective: to get you back into a stable mental and emotional state by returning you to the present. Remember: we feel pressure and react to it with fear when we worry about what the results of our work might be, or when we worry about repeating a past experience in which we failed. Thinking of the past or the future during a job can disrupt concentration and induce a counter-productive mind-body chemistry. We must stay in the present—and we can do that by remaining focused on our skills and on our task.

"Fear is based on getting stuck in time," says Thomas F. Crum, a stress author and aikido instructor. "We are worried about a possible future occurrence, usually based on a past experience, real or imagined." Lucinda Basset, in *From Panic to Power*, agrees: "Your fears may be about losing control. If you want to stay in control, stay in the present instead of projecting into the future."

Professional stock trader Constance Brown, a former world-class swimmer, believes that you cannot simultaneously think about the bottom line and what you are doing. "You have to be in the present to be able to win in the present. In sports, they call it being in the zone, being totally wrapped up in the moment."

Think back to times when you were focusing tightly on something in the present. Focus not only gets rid of distress, but also can mask pain—and even the weather. I jog daily and sometimes come home to chuckles from my family about running in the cold and wet. When I tell them I didn't realize it was cold and wet, it's hard for them to believe. But when I am focusing intently on running, everything else disappears. Other people report this effect while driving.

Whether it is through focus or deep breathing or simply stopping what you are doing and counting to ten, Brown says that in high-pressure situations, most people must find a way to bring their arousal levels down: "The more chaos we have around us, the more we need to develop an even greater inner calm to establish a working balance. If you decide to filter out all the distractions and tell yourself that you can cope with the market conditions, you'll be a much more relaxed trader. Essentially, if everything around you is stressful and you put more stress on yourself, then you won't be able to perform."

> ## The Importance of Proper Breathing
>
> Donovan Bailey, the 1996 Olympic one-hundred-meter champion, knows the value of proper breathing in tough circumstances. When his Mercedes flipped on an icy road and was destroyed in flames, Bailey escaped uninjured by taking a deep breath just before impact. "If I braced, I would have died or been paralyzed," he said. "I took a deep breath and relaxed like I was at the starting line at the Olympics and there's all that chaos around."
>
> According to former gymnast and stress lecturer Dan Millman, in order to master your emotions under pressure, "it's essential that you begin to observe and gain conscious control over your breathing. The unifying link between mind and body is the breath."
>
> Poor breathing can cause hyperventilation and irritate your emergency fear system. Sometimes you must force yourself to concentrate on your breathing to release the tension—breathe slowly and deeply using your lower stomach, then slowly exhale. Practice this before a pressure job.

MUSIC

Music is one of the great allies of emotion. If used properly, music can act as a bridge between nervousness and performance on the sports field, in the office or on the stage. Music can work in two ways: it can offer a soothing message to bring your anxiety level down or act as a catapult, turning your fear into extra energy or enhanced concentration.

Music works for a number of reasons. "First, familiar music is often associated with positive memories of pleasant experiences," Robert Thayer says. "Second, the lyrics of musical pieces may have positive associations with people. But beyond that, music reduces skeletal-muscle tension, especially rhythmic musical pieces. This is most evident with 'toe-tapping' music."

In our personal lives, music can be like a close friend we turn to for comfort, pleasure or escape. It is the mover and shaker of our emotions. And yet we have not fully tapped and organized music's tremendous power to motivate us to work better, to become more communicative and creative. We are just beginning to realize how much of an aid it can be in healing us psychologically, emotionally and even physically. In relatively closed circles—among athletes and music therapists—music's wonders are well known, but its secrets are often left to those who discover its powers through trial and error, or by accident.

Music evokes responses from the autonomic and central nervous systems, summoning adrenaline, endorphins and DHEA. Heart rate, pulse rate, blood pressure, respiration, skin responses, brain waves, and muscular responses are all affected. "Loud music has a tendency to speed up breathing rate [frequency] and to decrease regularity [rhythm]," says James Loehr, a counselor for athletic and corporate competitors. "Soft music slows the breathing rate and increases regularity."

Studies show that companies that use music in the workplace get 5 to 10 percent more production out of their employees. In general, the music elevates or enhances employees' moods, boosts enthusiasm, increases relaxation, and lessens nervousness. It also can mask distracting sounds, such as extraneous conversations and the hum of machines, keeping us on an even keel. In 1990, the University of Virginia reported significantly lower perceived exertion levels during exercise or work while music was being played.

However, the use of piped-in music is not always the answer. People's tastes in music vary and piped-in music may turn off workers who don't want to hear it. To solve this problem, some companies are experimenting with headsets for employees. A midwestern U.S. study looked at 256 non-supervisory employees who held 32 different clerical and administrative jobs, including data entry, correspondence, and account analysis. In the more simple and routine jobs, employees paid more attention to the music and therefore benefited from its mood-enhancing qualities; however, in complex and mentally challenging jobs, employees were more likely to be absorbed in their work and realize fewer of the music's benefits. Overall, productivity with the stereo headsets increased by 10.2 percent.

MANTRAS

As discussed in Chapter 5, we may sometimes need a cue word or *mantra* to snap us back into a desired emotion or frame of mind. A mantra is a technique of meditation that uses the repetition of a word or phrase, often spoken while exhaling. It can be used when you find yourself becoming stressed or find that your mind is wandering from the present. Some people use the word "one" or "now." Sometimes I use the phrase "My family loves me."

A mantra can be as simple as breathing in and out while counting the breaths from one to ten. This forces you to think of something other than distractions and returns you to the present moment. You can also use a phrase or a chord from your favorite music or song. When I am getting off track emotionally,

Music's Effect on Mood and Arousal Levels

- The higher the pitch, the more positive the effect.
- Slower music in minor keys warms the brain, which fosters mental alertness.
- Faster music in major keys cools the brain, which fosters a better mood.
- Classical composers such as Mozart, Haydn, and Beethoven tend to offend the fewest listeners.
- Repetitive rhythms such as Ravel's Bolero induce a trance-like state bordering on ecstasy.
- Musical rhythms liberate the mind from ordinary states, hence the popularity of music in religious and military settings.
- Music that gradually slows has a relaxing effect.
- The body's rhythms will adapt to the rhythms of live, close-up music.

sometimes I will hum—or just think of—the opening part of the 1950s song "Ebb Tide": "First, the tide rushes in..." Often that phrase, along with a deep breath or two, is enough to settle me down or, at the other end of the spectrum, motivate me.

VISUALIZATION

An effective technique to keep you in control and at an optimal level of arousal is visualization, sometimes known as *imagery*. Simply put, visualization is the technique of imagining, in detail, the progress of a particular job or sporting event. While visualizing, the subject sees the events unfolding from her own perspective: what she will see, hear, smell, feel, and do as the job unfolds.

Visualization, which can be used for both long- and short-term projects, can be a great tool as long as it is based on reality. I know some people who visualize only success, with images that are 100 percent positive. But life doesn't work that way, and we also need to picture the problems that are likely to arise during the course of a job.

This mental strategy has been used for decades by athletes and is now becoming accepted by a wide range of people—from professional speakers to neurosurgeons to managers nervous about firing an employee—as a method of preparing for a difficult job. Here, I would like to emphasize one of visualization's underdeveloped aspects: imagining nervousness in order to deal with it more effectively.

Visualization can prepare your mind-body for what is about to happen; in fact, it helps it to happen and it helps to keep you in optimal levels of arousal and performance. The pioneer psychologist Maxwell Maltz revealed that the lower parts of the brain and central nervous system cannot distinguish between something that has been vividly imagined and something that has actually occurred. In studying high achievers, Maltz discovered that when a person visualizes the routine of an upcoming task, all of the nerves involved in making a muscle move are electrically stimulated, although at a lower level than normal. Thus, a person will feel more comfortable when the pressure of a task is underway because he has been there before.

The medical profession is starting to embrace visualization as an aid to keeping doctors at an optimal level of arousal during operations. In a study of thirty-three surgeons, psychologists Terry Orlick and Judy McDonald discovered that 73 percent used mental imagery prior to surgery. Most would imagine the steps of the surgery, expanding two-dimensional textbook drawings into three-dimensional images of reality. They would vividly imagine cutting the skin and the fat and seeing the muscles underneath, rotating procedures to determine angles of entry into the body, and feeling the patient's tissue in their hands.

"My motto is to visualize," said one surgeon in the study. "I like to visualize the tissues in three dimensions and a lot of the time, I'll actually remember how it felt [in a past operation], how much I had to press and how much I had to handle the tissue to get to the right spot."

In keeping with my own belief that negative feelings and arousal must be anticipated, the surgeons would imagine potential setbacks during the operation and what the resulting course of action might be. Then they saw themselves overcoming the problems and bringing the surgery to a successful conclusion. "You can overcome just about anything if you're prepared for it mentally," one cardiac surgeon said. "When people come apart mentally, it's because they haven't taken enough time to prepare for when they're in there."

Office workers also need to visualize themselves overcoming problems, says Hendrie Weisinger, a clinical psychologist and consultant to Fortune 500 companies. "Imagine yourself struggling with

Personal Anecdote

I visualize success, but I also imagine pitfalls along the way. In 1987, I was told in passing by Murray Thomson, my managing editor at the *St. Catharines Standard*, that the newspaper had never won a National Newspaper Award in its one hundred-year history. At the time, I was about to begin researching a feature story on Hap and Paul Emms, a father and son who had coached successful junior hockey teams in Barrie and Niagara Falls and had sent many players to the National Hockey League. As an experiment, I imagined myself going through all the work required to craft a story powerful enough to win the National Newspaper Award.

I saw myself planning the story, completing the interviews, and writing it out. There was some potential controversy. Hap Emms, a stern disciplinarian and deal-maker, was not revered by everyone, and Paul had quit hockey partly because his father had "forced" him into it. Hap had become ill and might not be fully aware of the consequences of such an article. And so, in my visualization of the project, I saw myself treating the issues and the interviews with sensitivity, allowing for times of nervousness and arousal. Then I went beyond the writing of the story. I saw myself submitting it on the paper's behalf for a National Newspaper Award. I saw it being one of the three finalists, then selected as the winner; and I even saw myself going up and accepting the award. Events unfolded as I had visualized them, and I won first prize.

I still use visualization, but not for winning awards. In retrospect, I'm sure the positive thinking and the planning for good and bad bumps over the course of the project helped me to produce a better article, but ultimately we cannot predict how others will react to our work.

a task, feeling frustrated and perhaps pacing around your office," he says. "Then imagine yourself regaining your composure, sitting back down at your desk, feeling calm and in control. Then imagine yourself succeeding and feeling good."

Athletes are more successful if they imagine the strong emotions they are likely to feel during a competition, according to Bob Phillips, director of the Golf Psychology Training Center in Georgia. "The best way to accomplish this higher level of emotion is to be sure that you step into the image. If you simply see yourself doing the action, you are not really practicing the swing or the putt, and consequently you are not involved with the feeling as deeply as you could be. Make sure you are aware of what you see, hear, and smell in the scene."

Raising Arousal Levels

In pressure situations, most people need to relax and come down, not get psyched up. But if your level of arousal is not motivating you to produce, you may need to raise it. Consider making more projects and deadlines for yourself, thus adding some healthy pressure. Some people, especially golfers, use quick-breathing techniques to get themselves worked up over short periods or they use controlled anger (see Chapter 14). For more on raising arousal levels, refer to Chapter 5.

Raising Your Panic Threshold

Many people freeze or panic too quickly under pressure, partly because they are not exposed often enough, and partly because they have not learned how to deal with their emotional reaction. By testing your skills and tolerance under pressure, you can increase your ability to deal with fear—and the altered physical and emotional states it induces.

Instead of always avoiding fear, get to know it better. Raise your panic threshold by intentionally putting yourself in situations which make you embarrassed or defensive enough for your emergency fear system to kick in (see Chapter 14). Try these things:

- Drive behind the biggest, slowest truck on the road and refuse to pass.
- Stand in a long line at the bank and let some change fall onto the floor. Pick it up slowly.
- At work, put yourself in a position where you are the center of attention and speak to large groups of people.
- Be the office Santa.

But most of all, use determination under pressure. Become a *mucker*, a grinder who not only bounces back from setbacks and frustration, but learns from them and keeps plugging. Think of it as a chance to develop character.

7
Differences in Reaction to Pressure

"I love the fear, the risk, the buzz. I'm an adrenaline junkie."
—skier Tommy Moe, U.S. Olympic gold medalist

If you react to pressure situations differently than others, don't fret. Responses to pressure tend to be highly individualistic and people differ in terms of their receptiveness to various fear-management techniques. What stresses out one person may make another chuckle. A person may find something frustrating one day and shrug it off the next. Some people dread public speaking, while others will come off the stage only if they are dragged off. How we react to pressure at work can also differ from person to person, from task to task, and even from day to day.

Some people seem drawn to pressure situations. Skier Tommy Moe loves the excitement that comes along with the activation of his emergency fear system. "That's why I like high-risk sports. I'm attracted to the adrenaline rush. Fear is a big part of it."

According to Paul J. Rosch, president of the American Institute of Stress and a clinical professor of medicine and psychiatry at New York Medical College, "Stress signifies different things for each of us, and also really is different for each of us. The same steep roller coaster ride that is a terrifying experience for some can be a pleasurable thrill for others, or seem to have little effect either way. Stress can be the spice of life or the kiss of death—one man's meat and another's poison."

"Our fear systems are all unique and they react depending on our nervous hardwiring, our self-esteem, our upbringing, and our view of the world," says Karen Matthews, a professor of psychology at the University of Pittsburgh.

"Some people are more sensitive than others and are so-called hot reactors, responding up to thirty times a day [to pressure situations]."

Nature or Nurture?

In 1996, the prestigious journal *Science* published a study linking a certain gene to individuals prone to anxiety, pessimism, and negative thinking. In some people this "worry gene" is apparently shorter than in others, making them more vulnerable to fearful thinking.

Richard Davidson, a neuroscientist at the University of Wisconsin, has studied the activity of people's right and left prefrontal brain lobes. Those with livelier left sides tend to be more energetic and optimistic; those with more active right sides tend to be jittery and distressed. Davidson found these differences detectable even in ten-month-old infants. Those with right-sided activity cried hysterically in the first sixty seconds after being separated from their mothers, but the left-siders tended to explore their surroundings. "This might be one reason why people react so differently to circumstances," he says.

But, of course, environmental factors can work on genetics. A loving childhood can soothe a fearful outlook while a harsh one can nurture it and produce an anxiety disorder, according to psychiatrist Edward M. Hallowell. And our life experiences can also contribute to the way we react. For example, if we get rejected by a member of the opposite sex several times, we may become gun-shy and somewhat fearful of that gender, says Hallowell. A violent incident or accident can result in post-traumatic stress disorder or otherwise affect the nervous system. If you come from a more unstable era, such as the Depression, you may get the shakes just thinking about taking a chance financially. A relative of mine (in her late sixties) says she has never taken out a substantial loan from a bank "because I'd sit up all night worrying about how to pay for it."

Our experiences can also affect our self-esteem, and this connects with anxiety. "Generally, individuals who have high self-esteem tend to be less anxious than those who have low self-esteem," says mental health researcher Ada P. Kahn.

Hormones

Some of our pressure reactions are controlled by hormones activated through the emergency fear system. According to world-renowned hormone scientist Redford Williams, some people have a higher concentration of arousal hormones such as noradrenaline, dopamine, and testosterone, which tend to make their reactions more harsh, even hostile. Others have more hormones that tend to soothe, such as serotonin and DHEA.

Studies of animals reveal that the adrenal glands of aggressive species like lions have a high concentration of noradrenaline, while timid prey such as rabbits have greater concentrations of adrenaline, which in high doses is more useful for fleeing than for fighting. "But other studies show that humans have highly individualistic patterns of responding to [adrenaline and noradrenaline]," says fear researcher Rush W. Dozier Jr. "Players competing in energy-intensive sports like football and basketball, where emotions tend to fluctuate depending on the course of the game, have high levels of both chemicals."

According to James M. Dabbs Jr., professor of psychology at Georgia State University, trial lawyers, actors, and comedians tend to have high levels of testosterone, which make them confident, aggressive, and even domineering in their actions and thinking. Chemicals like testosterone can also be crucial in business deals, says Terry Burnham, an economist at Harvard's Kennedy School of Government who has studied why business negotiations so often fail.

Testosterone is a potent chemical released in fearful situations when a person feels he can dominate another person or a situation. "The answer, in my study, is that high-testosterone men are willing to walk away from deals that low-testosterone men accept, Burnham said. "Negotiation breakdowns of the sort that I studied are not supposed to occur [according to standard economics]. The role of testosterone in this area removes the paradox."

Other research shows that members of winning sports teams have higher levels of testosterone than the losers, even in chess matches. There could be a couple of reasons for this: the participants may be genetically enhanced with more testosterone, or they may trigger the potent hormone through mental techniques such as whipping themselves into a frenzy.

Beyond our chemical makeup, we are also born with genetic tendencies toward handling powerful hormones, says New York psychologist Gloria

Witkin. "We are born with a predisposed sensitivity to our own internal drugs and some people are better at using them constructively than others. Not everyone reacts to adrenaline in the same way, just as not everyone reacts to Coca-Cola or aspirin the same way. For some people, their adrenaline and other hormones react positively to threatening situations; it doesn't make them jittery or hypersensitive. Instead, it makes them feel good."

Attitudes

Fortunately, we are not jailed by genetics. Through conditioning, we can alter our reactions to fearful circumstances, says Witkin. In other words, we can train—to a point—our genetic tendencies. "We are all born with a different chemical makeup and different thresholds to fear, but we can develop our adrenaline system," she says. Sometimes, it can actually be an advantage for people to face fear and challenges early in life. "If trouble comes early enough, some people get a head start on facing challenges and they can develop their adrenaline system," she says.

This may be true of many successful men and women. In the mid-1990s, I researched the backgrounds of 500 high achievers—including scientists, entertainers, athletes, politicians, and explorers—and I discovered that 72.4 percent came from a home with serious parental problems, including 41 percent who had at least one parent die before they were twenty.

We react defensively to different things—in other words, we see different things as threats—because our needs and priorities differ. People who are materialistic may get upset with a bank clerk's error, seeing it as a threat to their financial standing. Others go into high arousal over a children's baseball game, perhaps because they are seeking to defend their kids against other families and blind umpires.

Gender

In general, psychologists say that men tend to be more in touch than women with their feelings of arousal and aggression—partially because of their genetic makeup and partially because they are exposed to roughhousing and competitive sports from an earlier age. "Women sometimes try to ignore problems," says Karen Matthews, "but men respond at work by trying to solve problems right away. That comes early. Boys are taught to be more active in problem-solving. It's a type of socialization." Women, on the other hand, are often sheltered from conflict.

Men may be more prone to act on their feelings and women more prone simply to talk about them, says Ruben C. Gur, a psychology professor at the University of Pennsylvania. Another general gender reaction, according to researchers at the University of Florida, is that in stressful situations men tend to unwind with exercise while women often gear down through social contact. According to a study published in 1996 by the Foundation for Future Leadership, a think tank in Washington, D.C., men are slightly better at handling pressure and coping with their own frustrations. Other research showed that because men generally have higher testosterone levels than women, they tend to be more dominant and assertive in the workplace. "Testosterone may make men more likely to assert themselves and more likely to strive for a dominant position," says sociologist Allan Mazur.

In physical confrontations men have a psychological, if not physical, edge over women, says Debbie Gardner, executive director of the Survive Institute in Cincinnati, which provides personal protection seminars for companies. "Men have an advantage because of what they learn during sports. They accidentally learn the things they need to protect themselves."

Some girls are encouraged to compete in sports and other areas of life while others are not, says Alfie Cohn, author of numerous books on human behavior. "Mixed messages are common, creating profoundly ambivalent feelings toward competition." In the 1960s, a theory that women feared success more than men was raised by Matina Horner in her doctoral dissertation at the University of Michigan. Horner believed that women were brought up to regard the pursuit of achievement as unfeminine and thus to become anxious throughout life at the prospect of doing well.

Age

Fear reactions differ among generations as well as genders. Many women of my mother's age never learned to drive a car, and are now too afraid to try.

Young people today may be less fearful of many things because they are exposed to them earlier in life. According to many psychologists, we often lose our fear of things by experiencing them.

Adults usually suffer more than children from nerves during a music exam, according to Clara Taylor, a music examiner. In golf, experienced players tend to suffer more from bouts of nervousness because they have stored up a larger vault of missed shots and bad memories, sports psychologists say.

When faced with a difficult situation, remember how individual your reaction to pressure can be. Many people need to breathe deeply and relax; others may want to take action. As we examine techniques for dealing with fear and pressure in the following three sections, you can adjust them to your individual personality and situation.

III
Focus

This section deals with the special circumstance of high-pressure situations on the job. In Chapter 8, we see that focusing effectively under pressure can produce some startling results and a phenomenon I call hyper flow. In Chapter 9, techniques for turning fear into enhanced performance are detailed. Chapter 10 stresses the need for a recovery period after high periods of arousal.

8
The Magic of Hyper Flow

"Fear kind of heightens your attention. When your adrenaline is flowing, you can work and think better."
—Terence McTigue, New York City Police bomb squad

We don't always have to be at optimal arousal to perform our best. Henry Muller proved this to the employees of his meatpacking plant in Niagara Falls. When a shotgun-toting robber stole a black case containing the salaries for the week, Muller was filled with fear. Rather than panic, though, he alertly grabbed a microphone and made an announcement over the public address system: "Stop him—he's got the payroll!" His men overpowered the thug before he could reach a getaway vehicle.

Muller's instant creativity shows there are times when we can transform the fear we feel during high arousal into an effective performance. But as we proceed through this next section, keep in mind that—as we saw in Chapter 6 —an optimal level of arousal is preferred for most difficult tasks. When we are engaged at an optimal level, we are usually in control. High arousal levels, on the other hand, can adversely affect our mental focus and our technique, especially when fine motor skills are required. In this section, however, we are going to examine those special circumstances when we cannot stay at optimal arousal or when we find ourselves in need of an extra boost for performance.

Focus: The Power of Now

With bombs falling all around them during the 1991 Gulf War, journalists Bernard Shaw, Peter Arnett, and John Holliman were sometimes forced to hide under tables in their Baghdad hotel. Nevertheless, they continued to provide award-winning television coverage for CNN. The trick, Shaw said, was to focus his fear on his job. "Fear can help you focus, if you allow it to. I decided to focus my fear on my job, on reporting what I saw and interviewing people and on getting the story out."

Under intense pressure and high arousal, one mental skill rises above all others: the ability to focus. If you can focus on the task at hand, pressure and other distractions can fade away or at least be reduced to manageable levels. At work, focus separates those who get things done on time from those who do not. In competition, focus separates the winners from the losers. Confidence and relaxation are keys to managing pressure as well, but often they do not fall into place until focus is achieved.

For many people, the ability to focus under duress is a serious problem. The greater the pressure, the greater the fear—and the greater the fear, the greater the distraction and subsequent negative emotional reaction. It takes much discipline and confidence to keep these gremlins at bay.

According to brain researcher Barbara Brown, focus without pressure and focus under pressure are two completely different things, involving two completely different people—both of whom are you. When you feel hyper or tense, it usually means that your emergency fear system has kicked in, your chemistry has changed, and you have gone into a state of arousal. This state changes your ability to perform—making it either better or worse than normal. In sports and business, for example, it is said that the peak performances are rarely achieved in "practice," when pressure levels are low. Sub-par performances are also common in highly competitive situations.

Focusing at any level of arousal can be difficult, but particularly so at higher levels, according to Robert Nideffer, a psychologist who has taught performance under pressure to the U.S. Navy SEALS, the U.S. Drug Enforcement Agency, U.S. Olympic teams, and business executives in Fortune 500 companies. "As emotional arousal increases through anger, frustration, fear, worry, or anxiety, concentration begins to narrow," he says. Such arousal leads to a kind of tunnel vision, which can make you miss the big picture. "The internal distractions interfere with your ability to read and react appropriately to the things that are going on around you."

The ability to focus effectively depends on a number of qualities. Three of the most important are:

1. **Staying in the present:** For example, when writing a test, thinking about how you have done on exams in the past or how you might be marked in a few days' time will distract your focus.
2. **Concentrating on your skills:** Think about the task at hand rather than the abstract implications of the work.
3. **Letting go:** Trusting yourself and your skills will allow you to get out of your own way.

These qualities are all related to one of my definitions of pressure: *pressure occurs when the past and the future come together to disrupt the present.* Staying in the present is the aim of focus. It is the power of now, of seizing the moment. If you are doing a complex task that lasts only a short while, the intensity of your focus becomes even more crucial. Positive thinking can help, says Terry Orlick, a consultant for many Olympic athletes, elite surgeons, astronauts, lawyers, and business executives. "Only by maintaining a positive state of mind and staying focused through the easy parts, the tough parts, and the turning points can we take full advantage of our strengths and live to our potentials."

To see examples of effective focus at high arousal, we don't have to go to a war zone. We need look no farther than our local hospital's emergency ward and operating rooms. Andrea Green, an obstetrician, says that she is sometimes very nervous while assisting at a difficult childbirth, but she pours herself into the operation so completely that she doesn't notice her nervousness until later. "When I'm in the delivery room, we sometimes have twenty seconds to make a lifesaving decision. After the crisis, I usually notice I've been sweating and my heart has been beating like crazy. While I'm in the middle of a tense situation, though, I try not to think about the anxiety but to channel it to keep me sharp." Green says she needs the extra alertness that comes from a pressure situation: "If you were just hanging out and being mellow, you wouldn't be able to make those split-second decisions. So to keep nervousness in check, I try to forget what could go wrong and focus on what I'm trained to do."

Focusing on your work may indeed be the best antidote to fear, according to Dan Millman, a former world champion athlete and college professor who gives seminars for educators, athletes, business executives, and politicians: "Anyone who has faced a moment of truth, who has felt the fear and leaped from the airplane, walked onto the stage and sat down to the piano or begun speaking to an audience, or otherwise walked to the raw edge and leaped, knows something that more timid souls do not—that once you are fully engaged, immersed in the activity, the fear either vanishes or fades, because your attention is no longer focused on what might happen, you are absorbed by what is happening. Fear may remain, but you don't notice it." Millman says that under pressure your fears may be in the background, in your subconscious, and they will help you focus even better once you get into the concentration mode.

Flow and Hyper Flow

One of the most fascinating aspects of intense concentration is *flow*. For years, athletes have called this "peak experience" or "getting into the zone." Mihaly Csikszentmihalyi, an expert in concentration and professor of management at Claremont Graduate University in California, is renowned for his research on flow. He believes that flow is total focus. "But it's a balance, really, between a total focus and a total release in a way," he says. "You are totally focused, but on the other hand, it is also happening on its own. It is like it is a total automatic process. The things you are saying to yourself throughout the whole performance are automatic in a way. They're the things that you've said to yourself over and over again in training. It is like you are taking all of the good parts of all of your training, and they are happening automatically."

Csikszentmihalyi contends that people cannot summon themselves into the state of flow by sheer force of will. Training is needed. If the challenge is too great, discouragement can set in. "Flow does not begin in the mind; it comes from physical or mental performance. You can't make it happen, but you can invite flow by preparing for greater challenges, removing distractions, and learning to focus. It helps to establish a routine. There almost has to be a physical ritual to achieve flow. Some athletes have a certain way of practicing, a certain way of tying their shoes before a contest." People in other activities can duplicate this by having a strict routine they go through while approaching a task.

It is difficult to achieve flow in a state of high arousal or by trying to dominate an opponent, says John Douillard of Boulder, Colorado, who teaches professional and amateur athletes and coaches. You have more of a chance if your outlook remains calm, even spiritual. "Flow is more related to Eastern philosophies such as Tao and Zen. In ancient cultures, exercise was a piece of a much larger puzzle. The original Kung Fu masters, for example, spent hours not to master the art of breaking bricks but to unleash their full human potential, to achieve what they called enlightenment."

According to Csikszentmihalyi, flow is more likely to happen if a person is not angry and does not let his or her ego come into play, but rather uses the activity or task to improve skills or meet a challenge. "Competition improves experience only as long as attention is focused primarily on the activity itself. If extrinsic goals, such as beating the opponent, wanting to impress an audience or obtaining a big professional contract, are what one is concerned about, then competition is likely to become a distraction, rather than an incentive to focus consciousness on what is happening."

However, one type of flow *can* happen under pressure. I call it *hyper flow*, and in sports there are dozens of examples, often when an athlete gets psyched up or even angry. Hyper flow is likely related to fight or flight, but it does not have the same big-bang response; rather it is longer lasting and more prevalent in mental activities. Isiah Thomas, one of the all-time greats of the National Basketball Association, said that some nights his anger "drove me to a high level of performance, but then I went beyond that into a zone of calm and peace. Everything seemed effortless. The plays were in slow motion and the rim seemed this big [he stretched his hands wide]. You are aware of every detail around you. You can even hear your own breath. It's a real high, like drugs." But hyper flow is hard to achieve and even tougher to sustain, Thomas added. "The next night, I couldn't get past the anger stage. It was frustrating."

As Isiah Thomas reminds us, we don't have to read comic books to find beings with super powers. We all have some of the Incredible Hulk within us, that mythical, mild-mannered man who transforms into a green superhero when his emotions are stirred. At or near its peak of fight or flight—in the form I have just described as hyper flow—emergency fear can help us create small miracles. It is a difficult mental, emotional, and physical state to achieve (we will explore some techniques in Chapter 9). What follows are some examples of the things we can experience when in hyper flow. These are not everyday events, but we should not call them miracles either. They are simply natural phenomena. If they do not occur often enough, it is because we do not know how to tap the substantial powers of the emergency fear system.

TACHYPSYCHIA: THE SLOW-MOTION EFFECT

Taken from the Greek word meaning "speed of the mind," tachypsychia is at work when action seems to happen in slow motion. This occurs because the brain is taking in much more detail than it normally does. Under ideal circumstances, tachypsychia can expand your ability to deal with time constraints. This phenomenon is reported in car crashes and police chases—and by basketball star Michael Jordan, who went into this state regularly when he got angry at opponents for doubting his ability. "I tend to take things personally," he said. I have conducted interviews with two hundred people involved in stressful situations—from car crashes to shootings to rescues—and in 90 percent of the cases, they reported that the action seemed to occur in slow motion. Alberta journalist Jeff Adams recalls how he was able to avoid an accident while riding his motorcycle on a foggy night in Wisconsin: "I was going sixty miles an hour when a deer leaped out of a ditch. I remember thinking of veering to the left, but seeing headlights from an oncoming car that were far too close. And going straight ahead would have sent me over the handlebars after I hit the deer. I remember looking to the right and deciding that the gravel shoulder was the best option. I leaned that way, while braking and gearing down, but the deer suddenly shuffled forward a step or two, just enough to let me slip by while staying on the pavement. I was so close, I could have slapped (the deer) on the butt. The whole episode was over in a split second, yet seemed to take several minutes. Decisions were made at lightning speed."

SUPERIOR CONCENTRATION

During the filming of the movie *The Sting II* in 1982, actor-comedian Jackie Gleason had a scene with Karl Malden in which the two men were to sink difficult shots on a pool table for $1,000. Producer Jennings Lang allotted two days for shooting and hired expert pool players to stand in as "doubles" for Gleason and Malden. But Gleason, an accomplished amateur player, deliberately put more pressure on himself by refusing to have a double. Malden, with the help of a double, made four straight shots into a corner pocket, then turned to Gleason and shouted, "Beat that!"

Gleason dramatically put some chalk on his cue stick, turned to the cameraman and announced, "Shoot me full. I want the camera to see my ball hit the other ball from overhead as soon as it leaves my cue, then follow the shot all the way until it comes back into this corner pocket. That way, the audience will know that The Great Gleason needs no stunt man." With heightened awareness, Gleason sank four straight shots, and for the fifth and decisive shot he departed from the script for an even trickier finale—a triple-bank shot worthy of any trick-shot artist. It went in, to the cheers of producer Lang, whose two-day shooting schedule had been reduced to thirty minutes through the excellent use of pressure. With his pride on the line, Gleason summoned the powerful ego defense and pumped his resources and arousal hormones into the job at hand.

ENHANCED STRENGTH

Lorraine Lengkeek, a five-foot three-inch grandmother, used a pair of binoculars to fight off a snarling 500-pound grizzly bear mauling her husband in Montana's Glacier Park. "I was so mad, I came in swinging and hit her four times," she said. "When you pick on my loved ones, I'm here to fight." Fight or flight can be an equalizer for the very young as well. Five-year-old Rocky Lyons saved his mother's life by pushing her up an embankment after their pickup truck overturned (she later needed 200 stitches).

OUT-OF-BODY EXPERIENCE

There seems to be a link between high arousal and some out-of-body experiences. Barbara Brown, a brain and human behavior researcher, proved that worry over what others think about your public speaking can propel you into a strange state of peace and calm—if you are well prepared. Here, she recalls her own experience after giving a speech at UCLA: "As I began to speak, my consciousness split completely. My perceptions and conscious sensations found themselves in a pastoral image, where I was resting on a green lawn under a tree, calm and totally relaxed. I was faintly aware that something related to me was on a platform and was speaking with words and thoughts, as if inspired. The separated 'I' had no idea what the other 'I' was talking about, far away. At the end of the ninety-minute speech, the split consciousness rejoined. I left the platform to considerable applause. It was quite possibly one of the best talks of my life." Brown believes that she was able to summon this performance by becoming aroused before the speech, then focusing on her work to such a point that she surrendered to her skills.

Patients who say they see themselves floating above their bodies to watch surgeons operate on them may also be experiencing a fight-or-flight experience, says fear expert Massad Ayoob. "The mind can create a false illusion in a hopeless situation. It's as if the senses are reaching out to get three-dimensional control, to create a graphic mental picture."

Overcoming Illness and Pain

Donald Cooper, a Toronto-based professional speaker, recalls at least two occasions when he was probably too sick to be working; but he persevered and was a success because he knew his emergency fear system would get him through it. "Before a keynote speech in Alberta, I had diarrhea and was dehydrated. I went three times to the men's room to throw up," he says. "As soon as my session started, though, I felt nothing, and nobody in the audience knew I was sick." Also that year he gave five one-hour speeches in one day when suffering from pneumonia. "Adrenaline (and endorphin) is the most powerful, phenomenal thing to prepare you for a crisis," he says. "But after the speeches, I crashed. The body can't function that long under those conditions."

In 1992 in Kingston, Ontario, Geraldo Zegarra suffered two broken legs, but freed his children from the wreckage of their van after it was crushed by a CP Rail freight train. In 1989, Calgary teenager Candace Middleton "died three times" after being pulled out of Glenmore Reservoir, but experienced no pain. "I felt really peaceful and comfortable, even though my friends were screaming," she later recalled.

Heightened Killer Instincts

Hyper flow and fight or flight are often reported in battle. The most celebrated hero of World War II—five-foot-seven-inch, 125-pound Audie Murphy—had deep insecurities left over from a traumatic childhood and being rejected by two branches of the military. Nevertheless, he single-handedly killed fifty enemy soldiers with controlled rage: "A demon enters my body. My brain is coldly alert and logical. I do not think of danger to myself. My whole being is concentrated on killing."

In his book *Billy Bishop: Canadian Hero*, author Dan McCaffery describes how Bishop used adrenaline-enhanced focus to force Baron Von Richthofen from the skies over Europe in World War I: "Bishop, spitting the putrid oil out of his mouth, was seething with rage. It was the first time in his career that he lost his temper in a dogfight, and that is what saved his life. He stood the Nieuport on its tail and zoomed straight up. Kicking the rudder bar, he banked over hard and plunged down on the red devil that had tormented him."

HYPER FLOW ON THE BOWLING LANES

To illustrate how fear energy can be focused into production, I introduce a story about a young man who made history by bowling three straight perfect games on December 18, 1993, while in an emotional state of medium to high arousal. (I am not recommending that all bowlers get so pumped up for a match—generally, arousal and delicate skills don't mix.)

To enter the strange and wonderful world of hyper flow, Troy Ockerman did some preparation. Prior to an important amateur competition in Corunna, Michigan, he got himself worked up at home by playing music on his electric guitar. He chose a fast, hard-driving song that he had composed himself. "Before a match, I like to get my adrenaline levels up," he says. "I try and get really hyped."

On the way to the bowling alley, the twenty-four-year-old amateur listened to a tape of his song until it became programed into his head: "Thump! Thump! Thump!" At the Riverbend Bowl, Ockerman got a little more intense when he read on the bulletin board that Wayne Bunce was King of the Hill for the previous month. "I got a little ticked off because I knew I was better than him. I kept telling myself, 'I'm tired of finishing second.'"

The ego defense seems to be a key part of Ockerman's story. He's been proving things to others for his entire life. In high school, grown to his full five feet four inches, he was too puny to make the football team. As an only child, he chose individual sports where he had only himself to rely on. As a teenager, after he rushed to the aid of two friends who got jumped in a fight outside a bar, he earned the nickname Taz, short for Tasmanian Devil. "The devil is short and thick, like me, with a big mouth, and feisty." (Friends say that, away from competition, Ockerman is friendly and laid back.)

Just prior to the match, Ockerman went through a ritual designed to get himself into a rhythm: with his eyes closed, he programmed his body for the actions it would need. He visualized himself walking straight down the alley with the ball in his right hand, keeping his body low while dropping his eyes to a spot two feet ahead of him, going slowly into a backswing with the ball and, after five quick steps, projecting the ball to the arrows on the floor leading to the ten pins. He also imagined how he would feel: "I feel my walk, I feel my arm and my release," he says. "I program the physical memory, the feelings I'm going to have when the pressure is on. Some nights I have poor concentration, but the pre-game mental programing seems to overcome it."

Ockerman was pumped up and tightly focused for his first match against Jerry Schulze. When Schulze opened poorly with a split, Taz's killer instinct surfaced and Ockerman immediately took the lead. Although Schulze went on to score a brilliant 258, Ockerman destroyed him with twelve consecutive strikes for a perfect 300.

Ockerman had something to prove against his next opponent as well. Jim Porter was in first place in this particular tournament. Taz kept his fast-paced routine going: one second standing at the line, five quick steps, high arm swing, and power and speed prior to releasing the ball. "People have tried to slow me down over the years, but it's a natural pace for me," he says. Between shots, Ockerman did not concentrate; rather, he walked around joking with people, tapping his feet and sipping a Diet Coke. As the strikes mounted in the second game, a crowd began to form around his alley and people were cheering for him. "I felt another adrenaline surge," he recalls. "Physically, I got stronger, my steps were faster and there was more revolution on the ball. It got more powerful as it hit the pocket. I had to be careful I didn't get too strong and fall out of my rhythm."

Ockerman stayed in his aggressive frame of mind by keeping his heavy metal song playing in the back of his head. "Under pressure, I tend to get myself pumped up for things. I think I'm more aggressive because I'm small." Porter tallied 237, well above his average, but not even close to Ockerman's second 300.

Next up was Wayne Bunce—the King of the Hill—who was still the favorite because Ockerman owned just a 216 average. But on this night, with Taz brimming with controlled adrenaline, rhythm, and confidence, it was no contest. "I didn't really understand what was happening," Ockerman says. "I was focusing so much, I was almost out of it. Mentally, everything was dead. I didn't hear the crowd much anymore. It was like a tunnel vision, a flow. Everything was flowing the same way that it had before. My timing was perfect. My arm swing was a flow. My confidence increased and it strengthened the rhythm, the flow, the tempo."

Although he described his state as mentally numb, Ockerman was more aware of what was happening in his game than ever before. "All I had to do was set the ball down on the alley and my body was perfectly programmed to do all the rest. Sometimes, I get physically fatigued, but as long as I'm mentally up, I can perform well."

Ockerman yelled, "Yes!" as the final pin fell into the gutter and his colleagues carried him around the bowling alley. Thirty-six straight strikes and three perfect games. Then, he turned white as the blood drained from his face—a common symptom of the fight-or-flight response.

I believe that Ockerman was able to reach a state of hyper flow that night because of several factors:

- He was aware of his sensitivity to adrenaline.
- He employed his ego defense by convincing himself that he had something to prove.
- He released the hormones of his emergency fear system with pre-match heavy metal music.
- He programed his mind-body with thoughts of his bowling technique.
- During the competition, he had intense focus for each shot, but he relaxed and let go between shots.
- He trusted himself.
- Caffeine from the Diet Cokes probably helped to keep his adrenaline levels up.

9
Turning Fear into Production

"The most successful people in business learn to convert their insecurities and fears into production."
—Donald Trump

As we have seen, focus and flow (or hyper flow) *are* attainable at high levels of arousal. Now we come to the $64,000 question: how? Simply put, we must turn our fear energy into production without allowing it to interfere with our technique.

The Two-Stage Rocket

I call my method for going from emergency arousal into a performance mode *fear-to-dispassion*. It involves taking the passionate feelings and energies of emergency arousal and inserting them directly into the task you are performing, whether it is public speaking, rescuing an accident victim, or making a last-second shot in a game. By "dispassion," I mean allowing passion to be transferred into the work and then washing your hands of it, at least on a conscious level. When this happens you are no longer distracted by or self-conscious about the nervous feelings. The emotions become dispassionate and are channeled into the task, making it possible for you to go on automatic pilot and surrender to your skills.

Using this method, you will sometimes be able to reach peak performance and enter what psychologist Robert Nideffer calls *the zone*. He recommends that people practice their skill under pressure in order to reach this unconscious surrender more often. (It doesn't happen all the time, even with the world's best professionals.) "It is through constant practice that you develop techniques to the point that they can be performed automatically, under highly stressful or competitive conditions. It is practicing until your actions can occur without any conscious thought that leads to your ability to enter the zone and perform to your full potential."

This fear-to-dispassion formula seems to lend itself more naturally to physical rather than mental skills. Pumping fear hormones into a physical task such as sprinting or lifting or fighting is natural for human beings, considering how we were originally programed to deal with physical threats. But it can work for delicate jobs, too. Bomb squad expert Terence McTigue says that you can even shut off a high-fear mode while dismantling an explosive: "But the trick is to concentrate on the technical aspects of the work, rather than on the danger. You suppress the fear, because if you're only thinking about getting your tail blown against a wall, you're not going to do the job correctly."

An orthopedic surgeon who took part in a study of medical professionals conducted by psychologists Terry Orlick and Judy McDonald (see Chapter 6) said that you can remove the distraction of nervousness by building up a rhythm in your task, especially if it combines physical and delicate skills. "You just have to keep going at a steady pace. To me, the rhythm is not wasting any moves. At the time of an operation, you don't talk. You concentrate and you look. That's where the rhythm comes in. You've been doing the hard physical work and all of a sudden you have to go from a grunting type of work to the very delicate, where you're passing wires around the spinal cord. Then at the end, it gets physical again."

THE TIME OUT

Many of the readers of my thirty-week psychology column on golf.com also reported success with this fear-to-dispassion formula—both in their golf games and in their business dealings off the course. But some had problems getting into the focus stage. Allowing a few seconds to pass as a bridge between the fear and the dispassion can help. Consider it a very brief "time out" that allows you to idle in neutral.

To shift into this neutral time out, you may want to use a cue word or phrase such as "Neutral" or "Let go." When you relax and let go, you get out of your own way. And getting *in* your own way (or trying too hard) is often what causes pressure in the first place. "Letting go" into neutral should allow you a second or two of distraction from the high arousal—just long enough to plug into your task. For example, if you are giving a high-pressure presentation in front of co-workers and you cannot get out of the arousal stage, stay physically present while taking a short time out, allowing your skills and training to kick in. Pausing briefly for deep breath or a sip of water can bring you into neutral; it can also return you to a more manageable level of arousal—what Robert Thayer calls calm energy. Then you can return yourself to tight focus on the job at hand.

Here is a reminder if you are having problems focusing: stay in the present by concentrating on the task rather than the potential results or past performances.

CUE WORDS

Cue words or phrases can also help you snap directly from high arousal into the dispassionate work stage—without an intervening shift to neutral. Focus on your task by saying "Absorb!" or "Technical." For example, if you are having a frustrating day at work and are running out of time, stop for a moment and remember that your feelings and worries are fear-based. Then use a cue word (such as "Adapt!") to get into the dispassionate stage. This will remind you to adapt your fear away from freeze or frustration into your work skills. Other effective cue words or phrases are "Stop!" "Get on with it!" "Now!" "Red!" and "Action!" The latter is appropriate because action gets fear out of

---

Exercise: The Two-Stage Formula

1. Feel the fear. Recognize your arousal as fear energy. There are no feelings of nervousness without fear, but fear is there to help you in a crisis. Feel glad and confident that you have it. It will make you stronger.
2. Change your fear to a dispassionate focus on skills. By redirecting fear energy into your work, you remove distractions and focus the energy on the task at hand. You may want to use a cue word or phrase, or take a brief time out, to make the transition. Trust yourself and your skills.

its freeze stage. Or, you may want to use a cue word directly related to the task. If you seize up while giving a presentation, that word could be "Podium!"

If you can capture this two-stage formula—fear-to-dispassion—stick with it. It may not work right away, or it may not work all the time. You may need to try it under various circumstances. Like anything else, practice can make near-perfect. But don't expect to plug your arousal into a task for which you are not adequately trained. You may be able to do it with skiing if you are skilled on the mountainsides, but not in acting or public speaking if it is your first time onstage. Develop your physical technique along with your emotional skills so that you learn to trust yourself.

If the two-stage technique does not work for you, you might want to try the three-stage technique described below.

The Three-Stage Rocket

If you continue to have problems with nervousness and can't channel it directly into your skills, here is another technique you can try. You can change the fear briefly into another passionate emotion—such as anger, excitement, or love—and then channel that feeling into the dispassionate work. This is my *alliance of emotions* (see Chapter 5), a technique that can be used for changing emotions over medium and short terms. But over the short term, while you are in the midst of a pressure task or time constraint, the transformation must be swift: *fear-to-passion-to-dispassion*.

The most dramatic example of the fear-to-passion-to-dispassion method has been seen in some police shootouts at the highest levels of arousal. The method is taught by Massad Ayoob, a New Hampshire police captain who is ahead of his time in finding ways to adapt to crisis situations. Ayoob has discovered that when a police officer is threatened by an armed suspect, the officer's emergency fear system kicks into high gear. This can hinder the officer if he has to use his gun because high arousal usually interferes with fine motor skills, such as accurately firing a weapon. "When you feel pressure, your whole body changes, and if you are attempting a delicate skill, your technique changes, as well," Ayoob says. "This change can make you start to tremble and it can make you seize up mentally." In too many gun battles, officers' accuracy with their gun breaks down because they are nervous and their arms and hands begin to shake.

Ayoob teaches officers to adapt their fear by turning it momentarily to anger and then just as quickly channeling it into their shooting technique. "Letting the fear turn briefly to anger helps that critical transmogrification. But because under the law a man in the grip of anger loses the critical defence of reasonableness, the anger must then be immediately channeled into a focus on dispassionately performing the indicated response."

Ayoob stresses that there must be a flow to the three stages or the process will break down. He says that such a formula can also be used by people in less-threatening situations. The key, he says, is for people to immediately recognize their nervousness as fear, then quickly get angry or passionate, then just as quickly transform that anger or passion into the act or the skill required by the situation. In the police example, that means putting all of the energy and focus into operating the gun. Adds Ayoob: "The focus is not on 'I'll kill you for trying to kill me.'

Personal Anecdote

I know that the three-stage method works in areas other than shootouts because I have used it successfully in running competitive races and in typing stories to a deadline.

In 1988, I was the anchor man in an amateur relay race in which each participant ran 440 yards. When the second-last runner on our team handed me the baton for the final leg of the race, I suffered a substantial bout of fear. I started out with a four- or five-yard lead on the other team, but suddenly my legs went numb. I became almost paralyzed with fear, thinking to myself, "What will my teammates think of me if I blow this lead?" For a second or two I was ready to quit, and my excuses starting flashing through my mind: "I'm out of shape," "I've had a problem with back spasms." Part of the problem was that I had never run 440 yards competitively. But that was not enough of an excuse; I could adapt. The only lame part of me was the way I was thinking.

I had to get mobilized, and I did it by getting angry with myself: "Clarkson, you idiot. Don't you dare let your teammates down. Three of them have put you into the lead position. Get moving!" That was a cue phrase to snap me into the second stage, and it worked; my legs started moving. However, my problem wasn't quite over. I was still thinking about why my legs had gone numb instead of concentrating on the race. I had to get into the third stage and focus on the process of running hard to the finish line. For a second or two I thought about nothing but pumping my legs as I had practiced. Then, I took off like a rocket—a forty-one-year-old rocket—feeling energized and yet strangely relaxed and in control. After the race was over, my teammates told me I had won by a hundred yards. I don't think I could have exploded like that without the boost provided by my fear.

For me, transforming the emotion of fear quickly to anger and then to a dispassionate response clearly worked wonders that day. I think it worked because I responded to the threat of losing by defending my team and perhaps my own pride. (Besides defending ego, the defense of others is a powerful force.) I didn't want my teammates and other people watching that race—including my wife and two sons—to question what had happened. So, it was the ego defense that produced my fear—which I then used as the first part of the three-stage formula.

The focus is on the job at hand: now is the time for Front Sight, Press [a gun term]."

Ayoob says that athletes at crisis points of a match use a method similar to the one he teaches police. "They don't fear physical danger, but maybe it's fear of failure," he says. "They learn to turn it into positive response." Although the ego defense may come into play as the motivator of fear, there is no ego in the endgame for a successful athlete, according to Bruce Ogilvie, a pioneer sports psychologist who has interviewed thousands of elite athletes. "In the moment of truth, they lose total self-awareness and even [experience] lack of consciousness of what's going on. They turn themselves over to their talent and their genes and let their ego get out of the way. It becomes an ideal harmony of mind and body."

For our primitive emergency fear system, the three-stage formula may seem more naturally suited to physical circumstances such as running and fighting, but this is not always the case. Shooting a gun has only been natural to human beings for a few hundred years, and it involves fine motor skills that are vulnerable to high arousal. I believe it is the training of the emergency fear system that is important here, allowing its adaptation to situations the cavemen never dreamed of. In at least two instances in basketball games, I have used this formula to achieve an altered state of consciousness, almost an out-of-body experience, resulting in remarkable shooting. I do not make myself out to be a professional athlete or any kind of a hero. I have simply trained and adapted my emergency fear system for present-day use. Like any new technique, this alliance of emotions needs to be practiced, especially the quick transfer from stages two to three.

Now let's examine the "passion" component of the three-stage formula. What emotion will you turn your fear into?

ANGER

In interviews with many high achievers, I have been told that anger is their best bridge between fear and the dispassionate stage. "Anger clearly mobilizes more fighting energy to an athlete or an actor or actress when he or she needs it most," says James Loehr, who has been a counselor to Olympic champions such as speed skater Dan Jansen and tennis star Chris Evert. "It can definitely overwhelm fear ... great athletes and actors have learned to move their emotional chemistry around to the desired direction." They often do this by getting mad, at others or themselves. "What, me nervous?" they say. "The hell with that!"

Dan Millman agrees: "Anger is stronger than fear and can be used to move through fear into action. When you meet fear on the road and need to get past it, get angry or get stopped. The choice is yours."

EXCITEMENT AND DETERMINATION

Anger is not everyone's cup of tea. You may find, as you practice and experiment, that anger (even controlled anger) is too explosive or repugnant. Instead, you may want to look at fear as presenting a challenge. Then you can use another type of passion—perhaps excitement or determination—to succeed. Instead of getting mad at yourself, you say, "This is it!" or "This is the moment I've been waiting for!" or "This is a chance to prove myself." Then, for the third and final stage, you pump your passion into whatever you are doing. It becomes, then, fear-to-excitement-to-dispassion or fear-to-determination-to-dispassion. (Some psychologists express it in a slightly different way: nervousness-to-challenge-to-performance. In any event, the same components are at work.)

LOVE

Love can move mountains, never mind fear. But if you need to transfer your nervousness promptly before a deadline passes, you may need a passionate example to think of—how deeply you love someone, or perhaps someone who inspires you sexually. Many athletes I know do that. Los Angeles cardiologist and stress author Arnold Fox says there are some connections between emergency arousal and sexual arousal, and one of them is how thoughts of love can stir your physiology. The technique here is fear-to-inspiration-to-dispassion.

Humor

Humor is another good middleman. Some people use it as a motivator or passionate emotion, others as a reliever of tension. Their technique is fear-to-humor-to-dispassion. On pressure-packed Wall Street, humor is a daily friend of salespeople and traders during moments of crisis. According to Frank Partnoy, a specialist in financial market regulation, much of Wall Street humor revolves around lines from the movie *Caddyshack*. Says Partnoy in his book *Fiasco*: "In the movie, when [actor] Bill Murray is caddying for a priest who is having the best round of his life, and a torrential downpour begins, Murray says, 'I don't think the heavy stuff's gonna come down for some time yet.'" That line was repeated constantly during the weeks following the peso crash." Partnoy says if you are planning to succeed on Wall Street, "you must be able to quote from this movie with great facility." After the quick laugh, of course, you had better be good at selling and trading.

Confidence

As I've already mentioned, I believe that confidence is an emotion—and a great go-between from nervousness to success. In 1990, I was pretty much scared to death as I stood outside the Grand Ballroom of the Palliser Hotel in Calgary, waiting to be introduced to Her Majesty the Queen along with more than a hundred other journalists. It was supposed to be a yes-Maam, get-the-media-onside bash for her Canadian tour. But a serious political issue (the Meech Lake Accord) had arisen that weekend and, because our political leaders had dropped the ball, all the journalists buzzed about asking Her Majesty what she knew about the issue. But I knew none of them would, since you are not allowed to ask the Queen a question unless she talks to you first. That's what made me nervous to the point of shaking: I knew I had to be the one to pop the question.

I changed my fear to the most powerful thing I had—my confidence—and it carried me through the handshake and the question, which I asked with perfect clarity ("What do you know about the Meech Lake Accord?"). To my surprise, she answered, but I was hustled away and the RCMP confiscated my credentials for the tour. For me, confidence was more than a state of mind that day; it changed my emotional chemistry away from fear. Fear-to-confidence-to-dispassion.

So, what exactly is going on in your mind-body chemistry during the three-stage formula? Here is what biochemists say happens when you successfully change your thinking from fear to anger or passion: the overload of adrenaline (which tightens you during the fear response) becomes overwhelmed or mobilized by dopamine, noradrenaline, and perhaps testosterone. As stated earlier, these three hormones are generally more action-based than adrenaline.

In the third stage—dispassion, or performance—a complex mix of hormones, including adrenaline, is at work, says Redford Williams of Duke University. But by that time you don't notice it. You can even be transformed into a type of auto-pilot experience ("the zone") which Robert Nideffer has described: "As your mind is free to focus totally on the world around you, time seems to slow down, and you feel very much in control." This is tachypsychia at work.

The first man to break the four-minute barrier in a one-mile race, Roger Bannister, trained hard for the event, partly driven by pride and ego, angry with those who scoffed at his training methods. He recalls his feelings as he approached the finish line: "The world seemed to stand still, or did not exist. I was relaxing so much that my mind seemed almost detached from my body. There was no strain. My mind took over. It raced well ahead of my body and drew me compellingly forward. I felt that the moment of a lifetime had come. There was no pain, only a great unity of movement and aim."

Exercise: The Three-Stage Formula

1. Feel your nervousness and recognize it as fear.
2. Change the fear to passion: anger, excitement, love, humor, or confidence.
3. Change the passion to dispassion as you focus entirely on your skills and your work.

10
Recovery

"If you continually put yourself in stressful situations ... you
need to plan times to rest and to recover from the stress, to
rebuild before you have a heavy workout again."
—Bea Cassou, managing director of corporate finance, Morgan Stanley
Dean Witter

After a period of medium to high arousal, you will need a recovery
period to bring your mind and body back to normal arousal levels. Few
of us can keep our emergency fear system in use or on alert for long
periods of time without suffering distress, fatigue, and perhaps even perma-
nent damage to the system.

In the three stages of stress, as touched upon in Chapter 1, the mind-body
goes into an initial arousal state. If the arousal is long-lasting, a second or
resistance phase is entered, in which the mind-body adjusts to the arousal. If
the arousal continues, the third and final stage is exhaustion.

After any arousal state, a recovery period is advised to get the system
ready for the next round of work. "Whatever your occupation is, you must
alternate between periods of performance and recovery," says Jeff Davidson,
a certified management consultant and stress author. "You're not hibernating
during recovery; you're just regrouping your physical and mental resources
and replenishing your spirit and emotions for the times when you might be
called upon to perform."

This "regrouping" can take place in the middle of the workday, allowing
you to continue with a difficult task after a brief recovery period. You can
even plan for this recovery time by not scheduling important meetings,
interviews, or jobs for the time immediately after the completion of an
important task.

"Sadly, many people don't realize how affected they are by stress until they crash," says Lauren Hanna, a Manhattan psychotherapist. "Making time to build in recovery is sometimes difficult and takes conscious effort and planning. When you find yourself feeling stressed, ask yourself, 'How have I taken care of myself today? What have I done to rejuvenate and energize my system?' It's important to check in with yourself and monitor your own progress. Think of your body as a gas tank in a car. Check your fuel gauge and if you need to refuel, take some time. You'll be amazed at how much better your engine will run." Hanna says that many people must remind themselves to keep their energy systems topped up with a proper diet and power naps.

When you relax your emergency fear system—which is powered biologically through the mind-body's sympathetic nervous system—you stop promoting the manufacture of aggressive hormones such as noradrenaline and dopamine and allow another system to take control—the parasympathetic system. Without getting too complex, the parasympathetic system is in charge of bringing the body into a relaxed state through the production of more soothing hormones like serotonin and endorphin.

Going into a recovery period after a strenuous episode of work does not necessarily mean you have to sleep, although some people may need to. There are a number of ways to encourage recovery just as there are many ways to encourage a state of high arousal. There are two main types of recovery: active and passive.

Active recovery can be achieved through exercise or a brisk walk. You can even continue working, but at less strenuous mental tasks such as filing, sorting, and making routine phone calls.

"Recovery does not necessarily mean that you must relax," says Jack Groppel, a lecturer and business consultant. "Recovery could involve paperwork, phone calls, etc. When and how to rest are vital to our well-being. The key to life is balancing stress and recovery. Without recovery, all stress eventually becomes excessive stress. Pure positive energy (or fun) is the single best measure of balance between stress and recovery." He adds that allowing for recovery time and mastering the recovery process eventually leads to increased productivity at work.

In the passive process, a break of ten to twenty minutes may do the trick. Other examples of passive rest are meditating, laughing, listening to music, reading, or taking a nap.

"One of the best ways to recharge is to sit still and do nothing, which may be torture for Type A personalities," says Kerry Crofton of Victoria, B.C., the director of a consulting firm specializing in wellness in the workplace. "But you must ignore the voice that tries to make you feel guilty for doing nothing. You are actually doing something—recovering. Focus your attention on the sights, sounds and smells around you. Tune in to the moment." Crofton recommends a brief nap after lunch—"it's part of our body's natural rhythm." She also advises recharging your batteries at the end of the day with a nap, belly breathing, walking, or listening to music.

Exercise: The Relaxation Response

Under normal circumstances, the body will recover on its own if given a chance to do so. In fact, the body has its own protective mechanism against overstress, according to Herbert Benson, associate professor of medicine at Harvard Medical School; he calls it the *relaxation response*. During the relaxation response, decreases are seen in heart rate, metabolism, and breathing as the body is brought back to what is likely a healthier balance.

Benson's relaxation response—an effective form of passive recovery—includes becoming quiet and passive for ten to twenty minutes and using a mantra word or phrase to keep your thoughts about work from creeping into the picture. Here are the basic components:

1. A quiet environment with few distractions.
2. A mental device. This must be a constant stimulus—a sound, a word, or a phrase repeated silently or aloud, or fixed gazing at an object. This will keep you from getting distracted and perhaps returning to arousal or tension. Breathing should be normal and regular.
3. A passive attitude. All thoughts, including those about the relaxation response, should be discarded. Let go of everything.
4. A comfortable position. This is to prevent muscular tension. It can be a sitting position or the cross-legged "lotus" position of yoga. Lying down is not encouraged as you may fall asleep (which, although it might be nice, is not part of this process!).

Adrenaline's Dangerous Allure

Some people are so used to—or attracted by—the so-called adrenaline buzz in their work that they rarely take time to relax and recover. If you don't shut off your emergency fear system once in a while, it can lead to letdowns in performance, burnout, ill health, or even a type of addiction to your hormones and the feelings they produce. Sometimes, that high you feel after you've closed a deal or finished a project can be alluring.

"Many of us get so hooked on that feeling in our job and even in our hobbies, it's hard to let go of it," says Archibald Hart, a psychologist and author of stress books. "You can become addicted psychologically to adrenaline and physically to endorphins."

This phenomenon manifests itself in a number of ways—just think about workaholics, or those who become obsessive about exercise. "If you come to rely on these things too heavily, you can suffer withdrawals if you don't get your regular *fix*," says Hart. He believes that your body was not intended to live in a constant state of emergency at work, home, or play. "If you do, you can produce four times more adrenaline than you should and some

---

Legal Advice

The following ten tips come from Mark Powers and Shawn McNalis. Together, they operate Atticus, a practice management education and training organization for attorneys. Although written with lawyers in mind, this advice can be adapted to many jobs.

1. Do not work after 6 P.M. or on weekends.
2. Stop over-promising to clients; force yourself to give realistic deadlines.
3. Create a list of tasks in order of importance.
4. Have realistic daily production standards for yourself and your staff.
5. Do not schedule every second of your day; leave spots open for the unexpected.
6. Work only with clients who meet your selection criteria.
7. To restore your energy, arrange a vacation or start an exercise program.
8. Write down everything swirling around in your mind so that you can prioritize and schedule things.
9. Hire at least a part-time person and delegate all projects that do not need to be handled by you.
10. Find a legal temp agency in your area, or sign up for an intern or a clerk.

people's adrenal glands actually become enlarged. It can lead to intestinal problems, blocked arteries, excessive production of acids, and ulcers, not to mention the psychological implications."

Lawyers seems particularly susceptible to the fear that underlies the adrenaline buzz. According to legal trainers Mark Powers and Shawn McNalis, many lawyers become dependent on it this fear. In a paper published by the Florida Bar Association, they write: "It can be fear of not having enough time, money or energy to invest in their practice, or fear that their practice will not survive.... This chemical support system was not intended to be depleted every day. Unfortunately, many attorneys live a life fueled by pure adrenaline and end up suffering a host of consequences, ranging from heart disease to high blood pressure." You can often tell if you suffer from this, they say, "if there is no deadline looming and so you have no motivation to work."

Perhaps employers should be aware of these potential problems when they make out schedules. Too much adrenaline is not only unhealthy, it's bad for business. Unfortunately, some companies hire so-called Type-A personalities—men and women who seek high-pressure situations. When they burn out, another Type-A is hired. In my own life, I have occasionally suffered from workaholism. Now, I must be aware of this and make an effort to balance my life, stopping for periods of recovery each day and during each project. If you think you are addicted to your own hormones, see your family physician for a start, and possibly an employee assistance representative at work.

> **The Don't Do List**
>
> It is advised that you don't do any of the following when you are overly nervous or tense:
>
> - Don't eat for a while. Your digestive system is shutting down.
> - Don't take unnecessary chances at work or at home.
> - Don't make important plans or decisions.
> - Don't provoke a situation which is unrelated to what is making you nervous.
> - DO identify the cause of your discomfort and deal with it.

IV
Mental Powers:
Practical Uses

This section will feature some practical applications of techniques for performing under pressure, fortified by examples and case studies. In Chapter 11, we will explore how to deal within time constraints and deadlines. Chapter 12 will tackle the well-documented problem of stage fright. Advice on handling the emotional issues involved in examinations and job interviews will be given in Chapter 13. Anyone aspiring to become a serious or elite athlete should read Chapter 14, in which the world's best share their secrets of pressure performing. In Chapter 15, fear management among emergency services personnel is discussed. The section closes with chapters on the increasing hassle of driving and how to deal with the pressure-cooker of everyday life.

11
Deadline Work: Creating More Room in Time

"There's a lot of give and play in the nervous system and we can achieve somewhat impossible things."
—Professor Mihaly Csikszentmihalyi

There may actually be a way to expand time in order to create more room for completing work under pressure. If nothing else, we can expand our ability to deal with time constraints and enter a world that sometimes resembles the cult TV show *The Twilight Zone*.

When arousal hormones start swimming through your system, strange things can occur. If you can harness this unwieldy force, time may appear to slow down and you may seem to have longer to finish your project. This slowdown effect is seen at the highest arousal level—fight or flight—in a condition known as *tachypsychia*. As mentioned in Chapter 8, tachypsychia is a valuable product of our emergency fear system, an effect created by the brain as it speeds up the body's metabolism to deal with a threat or heavy demand. Powerful hormones are released at a mind-boggling pace, says stress expert Massad Ayoob. "The more the danger, the more pronounced the slowdown is. Factors large and minute are recorded as the brain throws all its vast capability into the fight for survival, and because we are not used to that much detail being recorded by the mind in a short time frame, we remember it as if it had taken much longer."

In sports, the effect is regularly observed in baseball, where a batter has only a split second to pick up the flight of a pitcher's throw and decide whether it is a fastball, change-up, curve ball, or splitter. Ted Williams went to bat about

12,000 times against the world's fastest pitchers and learned to concentrate so well that he could see the seams on a ninety-mph fastball. "Somehow, baseball batters train themselves to make the ball seem bigger and bigger, even though in reality it's coming in as a visual slur," says Mihaly Csikszentmihalyi. "There must be something going on at the physiological level with hormones."

A milder form of tachypsychia seems to occur in less pressured situations. Most people have probably experienced unusually sharp concentration under pressure as they feel fear, anger, or excitement. I like to refer to this condition, when it is harnessed successfully, as hyper flow (as described in Chapter 8). The biology behind such a state is difficult to trace, says Calgary endocrinologist Alun Edwards: "There are hormones present in the brain we haven't identified yet. There are changes in the brain function, but we can't take the brain apart to investigate."

Experts are intrigued, yet science has virtually ignored hyper flow, tachypsychia and, to a lesser degree, fight or flight. But that may change in coming years, says Jaylan Turkkan, an associate professor in behavioral biology at Johns Hopkins University. "Scientists say, 'Yeah, I've heard of it,' but it's hard to pin down and study."

Many scientists and psychologists are reserving judgment on hyper flow until further evidence comes in. "It sounds plausible that we may be able to use it [consciously]," says psychology professor Redford Williams. He says it seems related to retention of details under pressure: "Evidence from research shows that rats which are shocked and stressed retain more memory. I think it has to do with rapid release of hormones under stress, especially noradrenaline in large releases." When people are emotionally aroused, they take in much more detail than normal, he says—and they retain those details. "When emotionally aroused, like people were during the JFK assassination, people remember exactly where they were at the time something happened. Memory laid down at the time of intense activity tends to be retrievable. It has something to do with intense activity of brain chemistry."

People who are highly trained in their jobs and regularly exposed to pressure (like athletes, doctors, and journalists) may be able to summon these special powers more reliably. According to John Krystal, associate professor of medicine at Yale University, "The system is sensitive to learning; it's similar to inducing a trance."

Roger Bernhardt, a New York psychoanalyst and hypnotherapist, believes that we can make more room for ourselves in the time we have for a job through a type of visualization: "Give yourself a hypnotic suggestion that your whole thinking mechanism will speed up so that the fifteen minutes available to you will be ample, as if it were a full hour."

But tachypsychia and hyper flow seem to be subconscious phenomena, and trying to activate them consciously may hinder the task, Csikszentmihalyi says. "It is possible that we could consciously use these things. But the knowledge may distract you from what you are concentrating on. That could slow you down and actually give you less time to respond to the task. You want to focus; you don't want to be self-conscious. It has to be automatic because it can accomplish much."

Under deadline pressure, we must stop trying too hard and trust our skills, says psychologist Steve Randall. "The pressure we feel is directly proportional to how much we're resisting what we're doing. It's similar to what happens when you put your index fingers into the ends of a Chinese finger puzzle [a five-inch-long, woven hollow tube]. If you try quickly to pull your fingers out, then there's some pressure and the puzzle turns into a trap. But if you simply relax, the trap opens up."

Mentalist (The Amazing) Kreskin, who is as practical as any entertainer, says there are two types of time: actual time and mental time. Mental time can expand and help a person deal with actual time more effectively. "The mind can alter reality and sometimes change the passage of actual time because of a need it has and because of the adrenaline. It almost takes you to a different world, or a different level of consciousness. We can use this period for examining and reflecting and making decisions."

Kreskin says that the subconscious mind plays a big role in helping us perform successfully under pressure. "We don't really understand that much about the subconscious mind. There are powerful things at work which can help us or hurt us."

Science should study concentration hormones so that people can better harness their resources, Kreskin says. "Only in recent years have we begun to understand the chemistry of the brain and what amazing natural abilities we possess. Under pressure, the mind can learn to do things that would normally take a lot longer."

My Experience with Deadlines

At various times during my career as a daily newspaper reporter, which began in 1967, I have worked to intense deadlines. At the *Niagara Falls Review* from 1977 to 1980 and at the *St. Catharines Standard* for much of my stint there (from 1980 to 1990), I was a police-beat reporter. Every morning around eight A.M., I'd drive over to the Niagara Regional Police station and get the lowdown on what had happened overnight. There was always something to write about. I'd jot down all the information in a notepad, drive over to the office, and start preparing the stories for that afternoon's edition. Sometimes I would have up to a dozen stories, and they would take some time to put together, especially when I had to conduct telephone interviews to confirm details or add quotes.

At both newspapers, my deadline was 10:45 A.M.—sort of ironic, because the code for a death on the police radio system was 10:45. To me, the word *deadline* added pressure. What happened to you if you missed a deadline? Did you get fired? I never found out, because in ten years of police reporting I was told by editors that I never missed one.

If I have had success, much of it comes not from some paranormal activity but from techniques firmly rooted in practicality. For one thing, I seem to be naturally efficient in back-to-the-wall situations (better than I am during times of no pressure). I think I was born that way. And I got better as I gained experience dealing with pressure in high school sports, which gave me confidence under the gun. I played hit and miss with mental techniques, including visualization, and learned to raise my threshold of anxiety. I also took typing in school, which increased my speed at the keyboard. I put all these skills into journalism, and they merged with the new training I received as a reporter.

In the following paragraphs I'll try to recapture a typical day of "making more room in time." One morning I collected several stories with good potential for that day's edition. The staff sergeant told me what had happened overnight: there had been several fender-bender car crashes, a despondent man had committed suicide over Niagara Falls, and a woman had been arrested for shoplifting in a department store. She had then evaded the store's security guard in a wild chase in which the guard jumped onto the floorboards of the getaway vehicle and held on for dear life as the car raced around the city, trying to shake her off. The guard stubbornly held on and eventually arrested the woman.

That last one jumped right out at me. I couldn't wait to get back to the office. Once there, I rushed through the door and announced to my editor, John Fedor, "Have I got a story for you!"

Fedor's enthusiasm was tempered by the fact that a few minutes before, he had received a telephone call from the suspect's husband and had assured him that we don't usually print stories about shoplifting. But now, all bets were off, and we decided to do a front-page story on the unusual case. First, I had to calm down to an optimal level of arousal to give the story its due—as well as to write the stories on the suicide and the car accidents.

The 10:45 A.M. deadline was not the only pressure. My excitement over the page one story became a pressure in itself; and there was the added pressure of getting the facts right. Whenever police charges were printed, you faced the possibility not only of hurting someone's reputation but of potential legal action. Remember, these were only charges, not yet proven in court.

Before I began hammering away at the keyboard, I went into physical and mental preparation, organizing my desk and making a battle plan: setting the order in which I would write the stories and making a list of the telephone calls I had to make. Then I went through a visualization process, seeing myself writing the stories and allowing for moments when things didn't go well. Finally, I visualized myself focusing more sharply as the deadline approached.

Before I wrote a word, I had my first of two large cups of coffee. That was my morning routine: two coffees and two pieces of toast. I'm sure the caffeine gave me extra energy, but whenever I had three cups, it produced some anxiety. With two cups I usually felt a little hyper, but it was a good hyper. (As little as two-and-a-half cups a day can double the adrenaline in your bloodstream, says Peter G. Hanson, a stress expert.)

It was 9:15 A.M. and I had only ninety minutes to deadline. Rather than continually glancing at the clock, I had a system whereby I checked the time every twenty minutes to see if I would have to adjust my work schedule. During each twenty-minute segment I disciplined myself to focus on the work, to stay in the present moment and not to worry about the time. I was confident and trusted my ability to do the job. Whenever the arousal, the confidence, and the trust came together, I went on a sort of automatic pilot—a type of hyper flow—and time seemed to slow down. I would look up at the clock and be mildly surprised that twenty minutes had not yet passed, only fifteen. Time seemed to be expanding.

(My deadline work wasn't always so smooth, though. Sometimes I would get a little frustrated by an editor's attitude or a cop's refusal to release information. I sometimes snapped myself out of this frustration by getting up briefly to walk it off or by quietly getting mad at somebody or at the story or at myself. Most of the time, however, I dealt with setbacks through sheer determination and an ability to transform the fear energy into a focus on my work, without thinking too much about what was going on.)

Suddenly I was typing faster. If I stumbled or became distracted or frustrated, it helped when I admitted that my frustration was a type of fear. I was afraid of missing a deadline, afraid of failing. By naming my fear, I was ready to deal with it. And I dealt with it through determination. I got on with the job, without worrying about failing. So what if I failed? There would be another day, another deadline.

On this particular morning, about fifteen minutes before deadline, I managed to reach the security guard on the phone, and she told me her incredible tale of holding on to the outside of the getaway car. I got all the details down quickly. A reporter sitting next to me later commented: "[You were] firing off questions in rapid fire, one after the other. I can't believe how you got it all in." That was just before deadline, usually my most focused time of the morning.

I know that other reporters also intensify their concentration as the clock ticks down. "As deadline gets nearer, it's more and more important to focus on the story at hand," says Pulitzer Prize winner Glenn Frankel of the *Washington Post*. "Deadline is really remorseless. You have to make decisions and you have to make them immediately, and you can't regret those decisions." Peter King of the *Los Angeles Times* admits to looking upon deadline writing as "a dread and doom," but once the process starts he welcomes the pressure because it forces him to "buckle my seatbelt and get on with the writing." Rick Bragg, with the *New York Times*, makes sure he focuses so much on the story that he forgets about everything "except going on automatic pilot. That's the only thing you have time for. You have to step out of your own way."

"Many athletes and successful business people are best when the deadline pressure is on," says Fran Tarkenton, a former National Football League quarterback who went on to found and develop more than a dozen business companies. Many football quarterbacks have a mediocre performance until the game is on the line, he says. "Their focus isn't there until the clock starts ticking down. The two-minute drill was my specialty, particularly later in my career, and it works through urgency. It forces you to focus on doing the things vital to winning."

Many business people create their own deadline pressure for heightened production, he adds. "Entrepreneurs are masters at creating a sense of urgency even where it may not exist. They do it by yanking out the safety net of the secure job. Developing a sense of urgency about pursuing your dreams of starting a business is vital."

These techniques work best if you are confident that your abilities can meet the challenge. Willie Unsoeld, the first American to reach the summit of Mount Everest, believes that expertise is a crucial component under pressure: "You need an element of risk, a challenge, to perform at your peak. The right amount of risk throws you into a state of total concentration where there is nothing but the moment. You feel as if you have more time and strength to accomplish things than you ever thought possible. But before you take that risk, you've got to master the fundamentals and become competent in the technical aspects of what it is you are doing."

After the 10:45 A.M. deadline passed, I usually became aware of tension and tightness in my shoulders. It must have been my emergency fear system talking to me, asking for a physical response, and I usually submitted with a brisk run or a pickup basketball game at the YMCA.

A final word: keep things in perspective. If you don't meet a deadline, life will go on.

Failing Under Pressure

We can't always control our skills under intense pressure. Just as the clock can be a motivator, it can also be a distraction. I know many reporters who are fine writers and interviewers but who perform worse when a deadline is imposed upon them.

None of us will always triumph under pressure. Remember my story from Chapter 9 about my brief, impromptu interview with the Queen? That was a no-no and broke the protocol of the royal tour. I rushed back to the office of the *Calgary Herald* and, after huddling with the managing editor, decided to write a news story about what the Queen had said. But the controversy intensified that night. I had been at the *Herald* for only three months and my probation was coming up. On top of that, my wife and two children had just moved from back east to join me. I was worried about them and also distracted by the moving plans. As I wrote, I became tense over the possible repercussions. As a result, I made a bad judgment call by bowing to an editor's request to give the story a scandalous lead: "How I broke protocol and spoke to the Queen." My training told me that was a mistake, even an untruth, but I went ahead and wrote that angle. The demands of the whole scenario had become too great for my resources.

Boy, did I pay for it. When the story appeared the next morning, all the monarchists in Western Canada flooded the *Herald*'s switchboard with hate messages. Even the Fleet Street papers in Britain criticized not only me and

---

Strategy Notes for Coping with Deadlines

- **Awareness:** Let your fear help you. Be aware that you will feel nervous or tense from time to time. Know that these feelings are natural, and remember that there is evidence that people can perform better under pressure than without it. If pressure is too high, examine your motives and expectations.
- **Management:** Prepare yourself physically (proper sleep, diet, exercise, job skills). Organize your desk and your work, allowing the proper amount of time for each segment of the work. Use your resources— talent, experience, co-workers, and physical skills—and positive thinking. Keep an optimal level of arousal by visualizing what you want to do, allowing for bumps in the road, and then trusting yourself to do it.
- **Focus:** Focus on the task, not the potential results; only check the clock periodically. Take breaks and allow recovery time at the end; no one can focus all day. If pressure gets too great near deadline, use the two- or three-stage formula described in Section III. Give yourself recovery time after high arousal.

my paper but all of Canada for suddenly becoming coarse toward Her Majesty. Time slowed down on that story as well, but in a different way; the controversy dragged on for weeks and weeks and became such a distraction that I found it difficult to write anything. I choked.

My point is that if you become too fearful and aroused, your performance and decision-making can suffer. Sociologist Carol Tavris, who wrote a book on anger management, says that if you feel too much pressure, arousal hormones can work against you. "Generally, adrenaline and noradrenaline help the brain to learn. As their levels rise, memory, concentration, and performance are sharpened and improve—to a point. If the body is flooded with adrenaline and you are too excited, concentration, and performance worsen."

12
Performance Anxiety

"That means if you're at a funeral, you'd rather be in the casket than giving the eulogy."
—Comedian Jerry Seinfeld's reaction to a study which showed that more people were afraid of performing in public than of dying

Within the human species, there seems to be no pressure quite like standing in front of a group of people and speaking or entertaining. Surveys show that public speaking is a greater fear for most people than heights or spiders—and, yes, greater even than fear of the Grim Reaper.

Some people—and they seem to be in the minority—thrive in front of a crowd. Victor Borge, the clown prince of piano-playing, used to say, "The moment I walk on the stage, no matter what my mood, if I have any regrets or feel sick or in pain, all that disappears. That is when the climax of my day occurs." But tales of so-called stage fright are more common, even among professionals like singers Barbra Streisand and Carly Simon, actor Laurence Olivier and former presidents Ronald Reagan and Franklin Roosevelt. Singer Perry Como seemed almost too relaxed in front of the TV camera, and yet he went through many of his famous sweaters because he pulled at the fabric when nervous.

Like almost anything else done under pressure, public speaking and performing usually turn out either better or worse than they do without pressure. We should be able to tip the balance in a positive direction, or at least take some of the edge off the pressure. And we can.

Before we go further, we should distinguish between information sessions (public and professional speaking and the art of giving presentations) and performing (acting, singing, or playing music before an audience). We will approach these two difficult activities separately, and yet my three strategies of fear management apply to both: becoming aware of your nervous reactions, keeping pressure at manageable levels, and being ready to respond to a high-pressure situation.

Public Speaking and Presentations

Most people who give speeches, presentations at work, or toasts at parties probably do not have much experience, making them more susceptible than entertainers to anxiety. If you have ever had to do such a thing, you are probably familiar with some of the feelings that occur when fear rears its ugly head: dry mouth, trembling voice, apprehensive thoughts, muscle tension, nausea, and memory disturbances.

People tend to be more relaxed when speaking to family and friends—even in large groups—than to strangers, according to fear researcher Rush W. Dozier Jr. This quirk has roots in our deep past, he says. "Anxiety about strangers seems to be an important element in the widespread fear of public speaking." It may also be connected to the fear of losing status within a social group—"a form of humil-iation that would have had real consequences among early humans, jeopardizing access to food, shelter, and reproductive opportunities." But these fears can also be learned, he says, from an insecure childhood, high parental expectations, or lack of experience in public speaking.

I have given perhaps a dozen presentations and speeches over the years, with mixed success. After reviewing my own talks and interviewing many experts on the subject, I have come to the conclusion that when people get too anxious before and during speeches, it is because they have looked upon them as performances rather than communication tasks. This viewpoint is obviously connected with ego, with worrying how their "performance" will be received by the audience.

Even professional speakers have problems with stage fright from time to time. Many speakers have told me that without their ego, they would not have achieved success; it is partly the ego which drives them to seek out their profession in the first place. But during a speech, ego can create too much pressure. "Most speakers with stage fright view speeches as performances," says Michael T. Motley, a communications professor at the University of

California at Davis. "They view the speaker's role as that of satisfying an audience of critics set on evaluating the speaker's behaviors—gestures, language, and eye contact." That is when the ego defense comes into play and the fear of a bad individual performance can lead to tension and flubs.

Those who approach a speech as an information-giving task have a greater chance to avoid this pitfall. In seeking to share their message with the audience, they take much of the pressure off themselves. "When you have a communication encounter, the speaker's role is to share ideas with an audience more interested in hearing what is being said, rather than how it is being said," Motley says. "The people really don't want to be analyzing or criticizing the speech. They want to learn something. Polish and eloquence have their virtues, but substance and communicative clarity are much more worthy primary objectives for the speaker. And they are also less likely to arouse anxiety." With this technique, I have discovered, you are apt to talk with your natural voice, making you feel more relaxed and less tense or pressured to entertain or be artificial.

Over the long haul, another way to increase your effectiveness is to hone your speaking skills and boost your confidence. And don't be afraid to fail. "We are all capable of developing better skills at speaking," says speaking instructor Peter Urs Bender. "We can all be more confident and effective in communicating our ideas to a group. But we must be willing to risk failure. We all experience situations where we aren't sure what to say. It's embarrassing to be speechless. Sometimes we try so hard to remember everything we want to cover that we end up forgetting everything."

If you continue to have mental burps while giving a speech or presentation, my techniques to alter mind-body chemistry can be helpful (see Chapters 5, 8, and 9). Reduce your arousal through deep breathing, the use of mantras, or with cue words or phrases ("Back to my normal voice"). Although most of the time you probably want to reduce anxiety by letting go and shifting into neutral before you resume your speech, you sometimes can use the three-stage formula of fear-to-passion-to-dispassion. While standing in knots on the podium you can think to yourself, "Dammit, get on with it!", and then focus on your presentation once more. And, of course, keep looking on it as a chance to deliver something exciting to others. These thoughts tend to bring on the proactive hormonal balance.

Exercise: Public Speaking Preparation

Speakers should remember that audiences have their own fears: that's why chairs at the front of a hall are often the last filled. "Plus, audiences actually want a presenter to succeed," says speaking instructor Priscilla Richardson. "It's no fun watching someone in agony." Richardson has a few tips:

- Use power breathing from your diaphragm, not your chest.
- Chat with someone before the speech to warm up your voice and relax your whole body.
- Use your natural voice, but don't be monotone.
- If your mouth becomes dry, press the tip of your tongue against the roof of your mouth.

Personal Anecdote

The visualization technique, used prior to a speech, can be effective on two fronts: for getting into a positive, relaxed frame of mind and for anticipating changes in your mind-body chemistry. I have goofed up in some presentations, but in 1993 at the conference of the Canadian Association of Journalists in Edmonton, I used the visualization method rather well.

I was scheduled to speak to a room full of journalists, who, as a professional group, can be among the most skeptical in the world. As added pressure, my talk was to be on my two encounters with reclusive author J.D. Salinger in the woods of New Hampshire. The subject was controversial because I had written a feature article about my visits and some people thought I had exploited the very private author.

Performing

If you stumble mentally or emotionally onstage, you have lots of company in show business. In a survey of more than 2,000 professional orchestral musicians in the United States, stage fright was the most frequently mentioned medical problem, with 16 percent reporting it to be a severe difficulty. Another study of 300 music students found that 21.3 percent suffered marked distress from stage fright.

Even world-class actors are not immune. "My courage sank and with each succeeding minute it became less possible to resist this horror," said actor Laurence Olivier of a bout of stage fright during a performance. "My cue came and I went onto that stage where I knew with grim certainty I would not be capable of remaining more than a few minutes. I began to watch for the instant at which my knowledge of the next line would vanish. I took one pace forward and stopped abruptly. My voice started to fade, my throat closed up, and the audience was beginning to go giddily 'round."

Hollywood legend Peter Ustinov said that frightening experiences can stay with an actor forever. He recalled his first acting part, at the age of sixteen: "It was an early version of Chekhov's *Uncle Vanya*, in a little country theater—a barn, actually —in Surrey ... And as the music for the overture, they played the 'Polonaise' from Eugene Onegin. I've never been able to listen to it since then without remembering the stage fright that I've long since overcome."

There are ways to cope with the butterflies of performance, some of them different than those for coping with public speaking nervousness. Studies show that the most popular methods musicians use to cope with anxiety are pre-performance relaxation and

I was quite nervous the night before in my hotel room, so I decided to visualize the next morning's presentation. In my mind's eye, I saw myself going over to the conference center, meeting the journalists who would be in the crowd, going up to the microphone and moving through all the points I wanted to make. Perhaps most importantly, I prepared for the worst. I saw myself getting peppered with questions about the controversy. I went so far as to imagine what my mind-body chemistry might be throughout the speech: starting out as medium to high arousal, then settling down as I gained confidence while talking at the mike. Then I pictured my reaction to the pointed questions. I saw myself getting a little defensive and tense but pulling out of it by taking a deep breath, keeping perspective and honoring other people's opinions, which would bring my arousal levels back to earth. As an added safety net, I imagined myself starting to stutter during the speech. I saw myself stepping back and apologizing for being nervous, saying I had recently watched the scary movie *Cape Fear*.

The next day, it didn't take long for the attacks to begin. It was about as bad as I had thought it would be as some reporters from other papers pounced on my Salinger story as exploitive. Sure enough, at times my arousal levels went up and down like a roller coaster. But I was prepared, and for the most part I was able to remain calm in my delivery. At one point, when a frog jumped into my throat, I cleared it away and apologized for being nervous "because I watched *Cape Fear* last night on pay TV in the hotel." The crowd stopped their hissing to laugh, and I continued without much of a hitch.

Another thing which helped me that day in Edmonton was that I looked upon the speech as a chance to share my experience with other journalists, rather than to show off. As it turned out, if I had tried to show off, I probably would have received a shoe in the forehead. After the ninety-minute speech, a big crowd of journalists came to congratulate me, including some of those who had been critical.

meditation techniques, alcohol and sedatives, and aerobic exercise. Some work, others do not.

TV host Sally Jessy Raphael is a proponent of visualization. "You have to imagine success along the way," she says. "You have to see yourself sitting in front of the camera. You have to imagine just what that camera looks like, what the set looks like, the color of the walls, everything. And you have to make that image very detailed and specific, so that you never go to bed without watching yourself do what you want to do."

As I said earlier, performing for an audience can be fundamentally different than giving a speech. Ego, flair, and a sense of the dramatic come into play much more. The character of the performer himself is often an integral part of the show—even the core of it. "For piano recitals and public soliloquies, one is expected to have unusual behavioral skills and to show them off," Michael T. Motley says. The performer gets used to working in this mode and generally is less anxious with it, he says.

However, many performers choose to shed their ego and instead *share* the music or the performance skills with others. Motley is a member of an amateur jazz combo that reduces its nervousness by having fun while playing, and sharing that fun with the audience. "A nice fringe benefit is that this not only eliminates our anxiety, but has improved our music." One night, Motley got so immersed while playing the blues ballad "When Sonny Gets Blue" on his saxophone that he got lost in the music and delivered his best performance. "Usually, I'm pretty stiff—the Al Gore of sax players—but that night I got into the zone of peak performance and I brought the house down," he recalls.

Reducing his ego and choosing instead to share with others also helped Les Taylor, an amateur baritone soloist. "Early in my career, I would get nauseous and shake like a leaf before, during and after nearly every performance. At one point, during a *Messiah* performance in the middle of 'But Who May

Abide,' I asked myself why I was doing this. Even though scared half to death, my heart in my throat, blood pounding in my ears, I continued, almost compulsively, to seize every opportunity to perform that I could. I was determined to overcome the problem."

The problem was that Taylor was worried what people would think if he made mistakes. "And if I tried to impose my considerable ego on the audience, the performance always suffered." After analyzing the situation, Taylor decided to forget about trying to impress people and, instead, share his music with them. "If I try to share what I love in the music, without getting my ego involved, trying to be faithful to the soul of the music, all is well," he says. "One either performs for self-glorification or as a service to others."

Another way to reduce anxiety is to remember that you love to perform and that you are ultimately doing it for yourself, not for the audience, says concert violinist Catherine Manoukian, who has held recitals in New York's Carnegie Hall. "You have to remind yourself why you wanted to do this in the first place. Once you do that, you just tend to forget about the pressures."

On the other end of the spectrum, there is sometimes a place for controlled anger in performances, says Dr. Don Greene, a former army Green Beret who has taught police, athletes, and entertainers. Greene was summoned by a New York opera singer who was frustrated by continually failing auditions. "Instead of telling him to park his anger, I had him focus on it," Greene says. "I taught him to 'center' himself on stage. The process cue (for centering) he chose, and which I supported, was 'f— you.' He imagined himself saying this to the audition panel as he introduced himself, and again right before he started to sing." Eventually, says Greene, the singer blew them away with his power and finally got his career going. "If you have anger in you, you may as well use it constructively," says Greene. "Energy like that isn't always available, but you must center (focus) it."

Shedding Your Skin

Some people overcome their fear of public speaking or entertaining by transforming into another person. Now *that* is changing your mind-body chemistry: fear-to-alter-ego-to-performance. Actress Marilyn Monroe became famous for this. Away from the lens, she was shy and insecure, with little charisma. But when the red light came on over the camera, something happened. Those who knew her said this metamorphosis was hard to pinpoint even if you were standing near her on the set. But the camera certainly picked it up, and it was visible on the silver screen. To people all over the world, Monroe became the sexiest, most charismatic woman of her era.

Donald Cooper of Toronto is one of the most successful and dynamic professional speakers in North America, giving about eighty talks annually. His basic message (that businesses and employers need to be sensitive to their clients' stresses) is delivered in a confident manner. And yet, partly to hide his two major fears, Cooper is not the same man onstage as he is in his personal life. Prior to a performance, Cooper is nervous "that I will forget what I will say [he has a memory disability] and that the audience won't like me."

Cooper copes through detailed preparation, by reminding himself that his message is more important than whether or not he is liked, and by transforming from a shy person to his alter ego. "In my private life, I am a hermit," he says. "I used to be pathologically shy. Even now, before I speak, I'm way too shy to approach a group of strangers ... but once someone reads my introduction at the podium, something inside me says it's showtime and the nervousness leaves." Back at home, Cooper sometimes slips into his alter-ego skin. "My kids will say, 'Is this Dad the Dad or is this Dad the Speaker?'"

In some types of performing, especially athletics, sports, and the emotional world of heavy metal music, anger and the ego defense often loom large, with some of the best performances being fueled by an I'll-show-you attitude.

Lukas Rossi doesn't think much about where his emotional drive comes from (perhaps from a dysfunctional upbringing), but he knows it is alive and kicking. Rossi is the lead singer for the Toronto band Cleavage, which was named Canada's top unsigned band at the North by Northeast Music Festival in 2000. It took the band more than 300 live shows (mostly in small bars) to get to that point.

"I turn into a different person onstage; it's like a mild form of schizophrenia," Rossi says. "In some songs there is a lot of rage; it takes over my body. I feel more masculine. I'm at the core of the action. I feel bigger, more important than I do [other times]. I guess there is a wimpy part of me and I want to defeat it. If I'm not pumped up, my performance will be no good; I need an audience; if there's only two people with a beer glass, I do worse; I feed off the crowd."

In the fall of 2000, Cleavage performed before officials from two major record companies at a private sitting in New York. To combat his nervousness prior to the performance, Rossi made sure he didn't dwell on it. Every time he thought of it, he looked upon it as excitement rather than nervousness. "I was getting this chance to share my music," he says. "I wrote that music. They were going to show me respect by being there. That's pretty cool."

Early in the interview for this book, Rossi said he doesn't get nervous and that he plays only for himself, but after thinking things through, he admitted that competition with other bands sometimes drives his performance to greater heights. "Before we go home that night, we have to prove that we're better than them. I know the other singer can't be as good as me. If people say you aren't, you want to prove them all wrong."

Rossi does not warm up the day of a concert. While other bands play, he paces up and down in the bar, nervous yet confident. Just before he goes onstage, he uses a type of visualization, remembering his best performances. It's a visualization not so much of technique as of feeling. "I feel the way I did at certain parts of songs. And I start to get that feeling again. Then I know the show will be good. I know the feeling is going to come again because it always does."

When he steps onto the stage, Rossi is tense and does not face the crowd. But as soon as the music starts and he begins to sing, he allows the transformation to come over him and he goes on automatic pilot.

If you've tried all of the techniques discussed above and performance jitters are still making your life miserable, you might consider seeking medical help, says Richard Rabkin, a Manhattan

---

Strategy Notes for Speaking and Performing

- **Awareness:** Remember that butterflies are common—and that we can adapt our fear into delivering a message. The audience wants you to succeed.
- **Management:** Check the venue ahead of time and visualize. Look upon a speech as information-sharing rather than a performance. Trust yourself.
- **Focus:** Channel your enthusiasm to others. Drink water and use breathing techniques.

psychiatrist. "Your doctor may be able to offer insights, stress management techniques, or even mild tranquilizers or other medication. Beta blockers have been shown to be effective for musicians suffering from performance anxiety."

13
Exams and Interviews

"My motto is, 'Pressure turns coal into diamonds.' When everything is riding on one moment, there have been times when I screwed up, but you learn from screwing up."
—Marvin Kawabata, student

I want to know your knowledge and abilities, and I want to know them now." This is the premise of exams and job interviews, and they can raise much tension in the person being queried. In some cases, a person's entire future can hang in the balance, and that is enough of a threat to set anyone's emergency fear system ringing.

In an increasingly competitive society, we need control of our emotional chemistry during school exams and job interviews, those ticklish tests of knowledge and character. If, under these pressure conditions, we cannot quickly call up what we know, we will fail—and second chances are sometimes hard to come by.

In general, a job interview or an exam requires an optimal level of arousal—calm energy (an arousal level just above neutral). We want to be motivated and alert, yet calm and in control of our reactions. We also need coping strategies in case we get too worked up or frustrated and our knowledge and abilities get blocked.

This chapter is not a step-by-step guide on how to prepare for and act during interviews and exams; rather, it offers some advice on how to approach them emotionally. When you are in the right emotional state, everything else usually falls into place—as long as your material is prepared.

Exams

Knowing that pressure can bring out your best during an exam can help your confidence, as long as you keep the internal pressure at a manageable level.

You don't want to put too much pressure on yourself by believing that you can deliver a perfect score; otherwise, you might choke the first time you meet a question you are not sure about.

Since a great deal of exam anxiety comes from fear of poor performance, preparation is key, according to Brian Poser, program coordinator of the learning skills program at York University in Toronto. "If you can test yourself adequately prior to an exam and go in with the knowledge that you do know your stuff, you might find your anxiety diminished."

The beginning of a test is very important because it can set the mental and emotional stage for the rest of the session, says Betty Poore, director of the Sylvan Learning Center in Ballwin, Missouri. "When you sit down to a test, take a couple of deep breaths immediately, even before you pick up a pencil. This will help you focus on the task at hand and take charge of your energy."

Sometimes we lose control of our emotional chemistry because we try too hard. Back in high school, I labored so hard in a typing test that I could not come up with an answer. As the clock ticked down, I became frustrated, on the verge of failing the class. At that moment, I gave up, slumped my head into my folded arms and sighed deeply. It was certainly not a technique I had planned in advance. Strangely, less than one minute later, I got into the test again, and suddenly my frustration was gone and my memory and skills returned. I went on to get a passing grade on that exam. That's a dramatic example of getting out of your own way—quitting—and I do not recommend it heartily to others. But I think it worked for me that day because I had been trying too hard. I completely let go for one minute, and when I did, something in my brain released the pressure holding my memory and my knowledge back. Now that I am aware of that issue in my emotional makeup, I can deal with it better when such a situation comes up again. It is one of the resources I realize I have in my repertoire.

Some students who become wound up find it helpful to set mini-breaks at specified points during an exam, Poser says. "They might want to close their eyes, relax their hands and do deep breathing exercises. Even thirty seconds can help bring down your symptoms of stress if you can use one of the various relaxation strategies."

If the above techniques don't work, it could be that your anxiety levels are too high on a daily basis. You are not managing your pressure efficiently. "Students do not have as much time to relax these days," says Michael Hooker, chancellor at the University of North Carolina at Chapel Hill. "They are not as comfortable with the world and their place in it. They work harder, are under more stress and have less fun."

Stress and pressure can be reduced through planning. "Pressure can be a good thing in small doses," says Jay Baglia, a graduate teaching assistant at the University of Southern Florida. "But pressure doesn't always come in small doses. Most students have a syllabus to look at for each of their classes all semester. It's all about planning." If everyday stress is a problem, it might be a good idea to see a counselor.

Counseling may also be advisable if exams produce such extreme distress that you become sick. "Some anxiety is normal in an exam," Brian Poser says. "To a degree, anxiety is facilitative of sharp concentration and alertness. When anxiety begins to impede your ability [to do your best] then it may be time to seek help. If you find your anxiety to be accompanied by headaches, nausea, feelings of despair, shaking, and trembling, or blanking out, it might be worth looking into services for reducing stress at your campus counseling center."

Exercise: Betty Poore's Eight-Point Plan for Exams

1. Take a few deep breaths to begin.
2. Study hard over an extended period of time, like an athlete training for competition. Don't cram.
3. Conceptualize, don't memorize. If you just memorize rather than understand, you go in feeling shaky.
4. Break down a big study project into small steps.
5. Concentrate and be organized.
6. Learn from previous failures and focus on the future.
7. Attack the test instead of it attacking you. Do the easier questions first.
8. Don't cheat. It will hurt only you and inhibit your self-confidence.

Job Interviews

For a job interview, you must prepare diligently by researching the company you are applying to and being thoroughly familiar with what the employer wants. But you also need to prepare your emergency fear system, because it will almost certainly kick in to some degree through tension or excitement. You can keep your emergency fear system flexible and in tune through the proper amount of sleep, a balanced diet, and exercise, and by keeping perspective and not worrying about things over which you have no control. Don't go into an interview feeling run down—mentally or physically.

Visualization is a good tool to use before a job interview. Picture yourself going through the whole process: showing up at the employer's door, shaking her hand firmly, sitting down, and responding to the questions. It's equally important to imagine potential problems along the way and how you will respond to them. You should also spend time thinking about what questions might come up and how you will respond to them (perhaps get someone to play the part of the interviewer).

Here's an important point on awareness: you should also *research yourself* thoroughly before the interview, says Dana Curtis, who works with the Office of Career Services at Harvard University. "Most people incorrectly assume that they know themselves, but they need to articulate to a stranger what he or she is interested in knowing about you. If you are not shy about discussing your talents and accomplishments, it may take some practice to sound confident but not arrogant." Curtis advises interviewees to think about the talents and abilities they possess, skills they would like to develop, activities and tasks they would like to avoid, the kinds of people and environments they prefer, current career and educational goals, and past experiences and what they have learned from them.

It is rare that someone needs to get psyched up for an interview; the pressure seems to come with it. However, if you aren't nervous, you may come up flat and devoid of the enthusiasm that most employers seek. If you need to raise your arousal level, look upon the interview as if you were an actor going into an audition or an athlete trying for a place on the team. Here's the formula: *disinterest-to-passion-to-performance*. (Try some of the techniques in Chapter 5.)

To make your environment as comfortable and friendly as possible, wear clothes that you feel good in and perhaps a favorite piece of jewelry. Such a memento can be comforting to touch if you feel yourself tensing up.

To begin the interview it is advisable to be in a confident, not quite aggressive emotional mood. Research suggests that most interviewers make up their minds about the candidate within the first five minutes, so you should start with a bang. Remember that if you are nervous, passionate emotions such as excitement and confidence can get you mobilized. Use the fear-to-passion-to-dispassion response. Think to yourself, "This is the chance I've been waiting for!" or "I've been preparing for this and now I will deliver." The emotion of confidence will carry through with a firm handshake, sustained eye contact and good posture. (You *should* be confident because you likely have more physical, mental, and emotional resources than you give yourself credit for. One night, write them all down.)

If you stumble and cannot maintain confidence, you might want to use a brief dose of anger ("Dammit, snap out of it right now!") to get yourself back in control. If you become tense and frazzled, you may want to take a few long, deep breaths, even if they are obvious to the interviewer (the fear-to-calm-to-dispassion response). Admitting that you are nervous and taking steps to deal with it might even earn you a few brownie points.

You can keep the tension and pressure at manageable levels by remembering that the interview is not a one-way street; the employer needs you as much as you need him. It is a matter of cooperation, not competition. The employer wants to bring out the best in you, so do not look upon the process as a confrontation.

Strategy Notes for Taking Examinations and Being Interviewed

- **Awareness:** Be aware that you will feel pressure and nervousness, but remember that these feelings are natural and there to help you.
- **Management:** Keep pressure at a manageable level through preparation, positive thinking, perspective, and breathing techniques.
- **Focus:** At times of high nervousness, use cue words to snap back to perspective and optimal arousal.

14
Elite Athletes: Raising the Emotional Bar

"The secret of great athletes is converting the pressure and their own insecurities into a powerful force and harnessing the electricity, the stress of the moment."
—U.S. track and field coach Brooks Johnson

Sports played for recreation should have as little anger and ego as possible. However, if you want to become an elite athlete and flourish at the top of your sport, learning to perform under pressure and work with your fears are musts.

As a general rule, high emotions and sports that use fine motor skills do not mix well. Who can forget golfer Greg Norman trying so hard to win his first Masters championship in 1996 that he blew a huge lead? And there are countless other examples of players in baseball, basketball, and figure skating getting so aroused that their technique fell apart.

But there is evidence that the very best sometimes *seek out* the pressure, using fear and anger as added weapons in their battle against equally talented foes. In addition, some top amateurs and professionals look for training and experience that can raise their optimal arousal levels, allowing them to perform more efficiently with high levels of fear and anger hormones in their system.

Processed properly, fear and anger are two of the most powerful motivators and skill enhancers in elite sports. But the techniques for harnessing these potentially explosive emotions are often discouraged and rarely talked about publicly.

"Athletes and racers generally don't talk to one another about fear. I've never spoken to another driver about it," says Tim Moser, a racecar driver, entrepreneur, and teacher. "It's one of those things that isn't discussed, even though I think fear can help your concentration and skill levels. If it comes up, a lot of people will tell you they're not scared of competition. Even drivers will tell you that. But that's a mistake. I think that means they're not in touch with their inner self and their inner feelings. That could hurt their performance."

Nervous feelings and negative emotions are often products of the mind-body's defense systems, says Yuri Hanin, a pioneer Russian sports researcher, now professor and senior researcher at the Research Institute for Olympic Sports in Finland. "It's a type of defense, a response to a threat. The whole person reacts, not just the mind or the body. It's a holistic response. The successful [athletes] are those able to establish a clear link between the uncomfortable feelings and what has triggered them, and then act on it." Hanin says that such defense systems can be genetic, from primal programing, but they can also be learned in childhood or developed through the world of competitive sports.

As I have researched peak performance under pressure over the years, I have come across some startling findings. It appears as though some of the most memorable performances in sporting history were fueled partly through the so-called negative emotions: Wilt Chamberlain's one hundred-point game, Jack Nicklaus's stunning victory in the 1986 Masters at age forty-six, and Carl Lewis' ninth Olympic gold medal in 1996. From golfer Tiger Woods to NBA legend Michael Jordan to tennis star Venus Williams, many superstars learn, mostly through trial and error, to turn pressure or threats into enhanced skills and concentration. Studying their performances has helped me to organize and fine-tune my formulas for dealing with pressure situations, particularly the fear-to-passion-to-dispassion technique. Athletes do get nervous and mad, but they learn to focus that energy on their performance. They are often rewarded with added quickness, strength, speed, and willpower.

Using Fear and Anger

High doses of fear and the subsequent arousal are best adapted to explosion sports like running, jumping, lifting and fighting. Fear helped Michael Johnson set a new world record of 19.32 seconds for a gold medal in the 200-

meter run at the 1996 Olympics in Atlanta. Johnson says much of the pressure was self-imposed, and it sent a tremor through his body when a race official told the runners to "get on your marks." He blasted out of the starting blocks .16 seconds after the starter's pistol sounded and thundered around the track at 25 miles an hour, eclipsing the world record by a sizeable .34 seconds. He said after the race, "There was pressure from the 80,000 people there who expect you to win, not to mention having the Olympic schedule changed for you, and all the years of magazine covers, photo shoots, people calling to try to take off the pressure but just making more pressure, and the fact that Frankie [Fredericks] and Ato Bolden were running really, really well ... I thought that if I didn't win this, a lot of things were going to be said that I would not want to hear ... It dumped a whole ton of pressure into the mix. It was like one of my competitors coming up and hitting me. It was perfect because I always race better under pressure."

Later, Johnson labeled that pressure as fear, and the race was certainly an example of the ego defense at work. But during the race, Johnson thought about nothing but his form and pumping his legs to the finish line. He converted his fear to passion and then to his highly trained technique of running. Remember the three-stage fear formula: *fear-to-passion-to-dispassion.*

It was not until the 1990s that some psychologists began to admit that the so-called negative emotions of fear and anger do sometimes have a place in sports. Those emotions produce the biggest hormonal bangs, according to Yuri Hanin. "Anger, aggression, fear, and anxiety can produce some big performances, if they are focused properly," Hanin says. "High-level mobilizing energy comes from negative emotions. They are often untouched reserves. Positive emotions [joy, contentment] are not as quick to act or as intensive as negative emotions. Not all athletes are ready for competitions because they don't have enough negatives, or they don't channel or allocate them in the right way." About 40 percent of elite athletes need a high level of pre-competition anxiety to perform well, according to Hanin. "They are more efficient when they're tense or nervous. That's helpful to them."

Former U.S. Olympic women's track and field coach Brooks Johnson says the best athletes learn to change their fear and anger into potent forces. "Some people are able to take the negative feelings and convert them into energy and better focus," he says. "It creates this sort of electricity and they take it and focus it on their event. Bill Russell got so nervous before [NBA] games, he'd lose his lunch, then he'd go out and turn that nervousness into a marvelous performance. It's Ying and Yang, an awesome pressure. All the great ones have the ability to do this. You cannot get to a certain level without this mentality."

"In football, you can play in a rage," says former NFL player Tom Jackson, now an analyst for ESPN. "Before the game, I would be so emotional, I would be crying. But there has to be a sort of calculation to your rage. You can't be just running around. You have to focus it." Jackson says it's more difficult to play with high emotion when you are an offensive football player, particularly a quarterback, because high arousal can impair judgment and the ability to see the big picture on the field.

One would think that strong emotions and baseball batting would not go hand in hand. But on September 17, 1997, Mo Vaughn of the Boston Red Sox seemed to invoke emergency fear hormones in a game against the Toronto Blue Jays. Before the game, the media and the Boston fans had turned on big Mo because he had openly slammed Red Sox management over their handling of his contract negotiations. As the fans booed, Vaughn smacked two home runs to give Boston a 4-3 victory. "Mo's a very emotional person," teammate John Valentin said after the game. "He lives and dies for this city. I think he's a little hurt with the way things are going."

David Pargman, a sports psychologist at Florida State University, says that tennis greats Jimmy Connors and John McEnroe have used strategic anger and even temper for crucial parts of a match. "The world may see a spoiled brat, but some elite athletes turn on the anger strategically," he says.

Many elite athletes don't even wait for the pressure of a match to embrace them; they deliberately raise their emergency fear system. Simple thoughts can do the trick, and some of them are not pretty. Pioneer sports psychologist Bruce Ogilvie knew of a defensive end in the National Football League who got himself psyched up for several days before an important game by pretending the opponent he would be facing had raped his wife.

Paul Albert, a New York librarian training to become a professional cyclist, draws up a personal *enemies list* to get him psyched for better times in his races. "I look on (the races) as an epic challenge, perhaps me against the kids who pushed me around in junior high," he says. "As I think about that and start to visualize my race, it's like I can walk through a wall."

The Ego Defense

The ego defense is a lethal weapon used by many top performers, including some that sports fans might not associate with huge ego, like hockey's Wayne Gretzky and Michael Jordan and Larry Bird of the NBA. These three often performed best when they defended themselves against what they saw as personal attacks.

In 1993, columnist Bob McKenzie of the *Toronto Star* wrote that The Great Gretzky had played poorly as his Los Angeles Kings fell behind three games to two to the Toronto Maple Leafs in the Eastern Conference finals of the National Hockey League playoffs. Gretzky admitted he felt insulted by the column and used it for motivation to score the winning goal in Game 6. Then, he played one of his finest games as the Kings won Game 7. In the next series Los Angeles lost the Stanley Cup finals, but McKenzie said, "I thought to myself, if L.A. had won the cup, they should have put my name on it along with the winning players. We've all heard about the power of the press, but that was ridiculous."

Gretzky's coach with the Edmonton Oilers, Glen Sather, said that hockey "was more than a game to him. Wayne channeled his anger very well, but he didn't outwardly expose himself to the public. If somebody said something about him being a whiner, he got really ticked. It was purely a pride thing."

Michael Jordan: A Master of Controlled Emotion

Michael Jordan of the Chicago Bulls went into high-arousal mode to strike down both his critics and his opponents on his way to winning six NBA championships. He often berated opponents to get himself worked up, and his controlled anger gave him added quickness and concentration and better shooting.

In two years of covering the NBA, I studied Jordan closely. Most people see him simply as one of the most talented basketball players of all time, but he is more than that: Jordan takes the use of controlled emotions to the stratosphere. I have interviewed Jordan, but I don't think he can explain his technique; I think he learned it through trial and error. I believe he uses emotions in two ways: through his worry system, which makes him practice harder than his opponents to overcome his weaknesses and improve his outside shooting, and also by trash-talking during games.

There is no doubt that fear is one of the biggest motivators for Jordan. "I tend to take things personally," he says. "My challenge has always been to never give people room for any conversation about my abilities. Everyone's looking for just one little slip-up so they can create a big hole in my game. And whenever I see that, I work to close that as quickly as possible. People will say that [Scottie] Pippen's the best player on this team or Penny Hardaway's the best player in the East or Hakeem Olajuwon or Shaq are the best players in the game. Well, I stopped all that conversation. The bottom line is, while I'm still on the court, don't try to move anyone into my spot. I'm the only one who will decide that. Only me."

Clinical psychologist Robert W. Grant calls this partly overcompensating for an insecurity, and he says it is rampant in the elite sports world.

Many elite athletes use anger as a bridge from the ego defense to performance mode. Minutes before he smacked the game-winning homer in the 1986 World Series, Kirk Gibson was sitting lame in the locker room, hobbled by several injuries. But when he heard TV commentator Vin Scully announce that he would not be able to pinch-hit, Gibson became inflamed. "That's it!" he shouted, then came out of the dugout and turned his anger against the opposing pitcher.

It sounds simple, doesn't it?—turning the feelings inspired by the ego defense into your performance. But at the critical moment, successful athletes actually shut their feelings down, or redirect them into the mechanics of their sport. Unheralded Mike Powell turned this trick to smash a world record which was thought to be untouchable: Bob Beamon's long-jump mark of 29 feet, 2.5 inches set in 1968. At the world track and field championships in Toyko in 1991, only superstar Carl Lewis was thought to have a chance to break the record, and that got Powell angry. "I was really mad and angry that everybody was counting me out," said Powell, who had lost nine consecutive times to Lewis. "It was a personal insult. I'd show them."

Prior to the key jump, Powell visualized everything: "I knew in my mind what was going to happen. It was eerie. I saw it all in my mind like precognition: the good speed on the runway, the good timing and good takeoff on the board, that super extra burst of strength. It felt like it was supposed to happen."

Powell turned off his ego as he made his leap, and he seemed to enter a slow-motion world of hyper flow. "It all happened in slow motion," he recalls.

"I can remember every movement of my body, especially when I was in the air. In the air I remember thinking, 'Soon I'll be hitting the sand and the crowd will go OOOH! and then it will announced that I've broken the record.'" That is the way it turned out as Powell soared 29 feet, 4.5 inches.

Optimal Arousal

I have devoted nearly this entire chapter to the use of so-called negative emotions for high performance. I have done this because the role of fear, anger, and ego in peak sports performances is rarely documented. Nevertheless, I must now state that, after coaching and playing at a high amateur level for three decades and covering professional sports as a reporter for many years, I believe that fear and anger should be saved for special circumstances.

Many, if not most, sports coaches and psychologists discourage the use of anger. "Usually, anger leads to inconsistent results," says sports psychologist Jerry May of the University of Nevada at Reno. "Anger can tighten muscles and increase the risk of injury. To respond optimally, to excel, you must be excited but relaxed."

In the main, the best way for elite athletes to prepare for games and to play them is through an optimal level of arousal; in other

Optimal Arousal Level According to Skill Performed

5 (extremely excited): football blocking and tackling, 220-yard and 440-yard runs, weightlifting, push-ups, sit-ups, bent-arm hang test

4 (somewhat excited): running long jump, running very short and long races, shot putt, swimming races, wrestling, judo

3 (aroused but not excited): most basketball skills, boxing, high jumping, most gymnastic skills, most soccer skills

2 (somewhat aroused): baseball pitching and hitting, fancy diving, fencing, football quarterbacking, tennis

1 (slightly aroused): archery, bowling, basketball free throws, football field-goal kicking, golf putting and short irons, skating figure eights

0 (normal state)

words, a level at which the arousal is manageable for the athlete. Some people call this the optimal part of the arousal curve. If an athlete gets too aroused and goes beyond the curve, mechanics often break down. John Anderson, a sports psychologist who works with U.S. Olympic athletes, says, "You may discover you can learn to handle 6 out of 10 on the [arousal] scale, but if you go beyond that and you haven't been there before, you begin to worry. Then you forget to trust your internal system and [you begin to] focus on external things. Then the arousal state is not functional." To get to their optimal level, some athletes will have to get more aroused while others may have to relax and come down. To accomplish the latter, many athletes use deep breathing, visualization techniques, or meditation. Golfer Lee Trevino uses humor. To maintain the desired level of arousal, many athletes use their favorite music before a performance, or they think of music during crucial parts of the performance. Many athletes think of their spouse or children when they need to become motivated or centered, as Juli Inkster did in winning the 1999 U.S. women's open golf championship or as Lance Armstrong did to win the Tour de France the same year.

Many serious athletes have learned to raise their levels of optimal arousal to the point where they are performing at a higher arousal level than their competitors, giving them a decided edge over the long haul. For example, let's say a hockey player can perform well at a level of 3 out of 5 on an arousal scale; he may be able to increase that to 4, thus allowing more arousal hormones

A Word About Joy

Writers who follow baseball closely believe that the emotion of joy was one of the forces which propelled the fabulous home run derby between Mark McGwire of the St. Louis Cardinals (who had 70) and Sammy Sosa of the Chicago Cubs (who hit 66) in 1998. Both broke Roger Maris's hallowed mark of 61, despite increasing media and fan pressure late in the season.

McGwire admitted he'd had emotional problems in the past, but after seeing a psychotherapist, he was in a proactive state of mind all season. McGwire said that the reasons for his record were his strong mind, positive thinking, a willingness to embrace the media pressure, and the excitement of the race against Sosa. Rather than worry about breaking the record, McGwire said he looked upon it as a challenge, as excitement.

to help him. John Anderson says that some world-class athletes have learned to perform at a level of 10 out of 10. "They learn to trust their performance system under high arousal, and it gives them an added boost. And they learn that their feelings of nervousness are often a good sign."

Kirk Gibson says young athletes must get used to pressure to have a realistic chance of making it big. "Playing in the big games is one thing, but you have to create some pressure in practice, too. Always have something on the line, even when you're practicing by yourself. You have to learn to become tough. That way, when the big moment comes, you know the feelings, and you can learn to deal with even more intense feelings."

Strategy Notes for Improving Athletic Performance

- **Awareness:** Be aware that high emotions and sports with fine motor skills are generally not compatible, although arousal can increase effort and willpower.
- **Management:** Keep expectations reasonable. With training and experience, especially under pressure, you can raise your optimal level of arousal. Trust yourself. If tense, force yourself to concentrate on your breathing—breathe slowly and deeply using your lower stomach, then slowly exhale.
- **Focus:** Convert your controlled fear and anger into added electricity for special times in a match. Visualize.

15
Fear Energy in the Emergency Services

"You can turn a high-stress situation to your advantage, make it
part of the solution as opposed to part of the problem."
—firefighter Stephen Ruda

mergency services personnel—police, firefighters, paramedics, and
soldiers—have a more difficult job than we realize. Not only do they
have to deal with pressure situations (even life-and-death ones) and
victims' reactions to those situations, they are also faced with their own reactions to pressure and fear.

"I've faced the devil," says Captain Stephen Ruda of the Los Angeles Fire
Department, explaining the stress of his job and the uncertainties of dealing
with fear—his own and other people's. "When you go into a fight-or-flight
mode and you have to make a split-second decision, you had better hope that
you have been trained properly to deal with such high levels of stress." Ruda
says his department has such training procedures, but many other emergency
services groups do not. They may be trained in the handling of guns, chainsaws, and fire hoses under relaxed training conditions—but handling such
potent, delicate implements under duress is quite another matter.

"There is a problem with firefighter training in the U.S. in that state and
federal agencies don't allow us to hold realistic training any more," says Judy
Carr, an instructor for H.K. Carr and Associates in Englishtown, New Jersey,
which trains firefighters, police, and other emergency response teams. In
practice sessions, old houses and real fires can no longer be used; they have
been replaced by unrealistic simulations and propane. "It's hard to take our
students to the edge of arousal, so they are not prepared for it when the real
thing happens," Carr says. "You can't raise people's panic thresholds under

poor training conditions. Using propane, which you can shut down anytime, gives students a false sense of protection."

Many police departments report the same problem. Police officers not only protect the public, often they must protect themselves from harm. And in doing that, they sometimes shoot innocent people because they cannot control their fear response or are startled by it. In 1993, an innocent person was killed by police bullets because the Denver police were not adequately trained to deal with a high-stress shooting. That ruling was made by a jury and upheld by the U.S. Court of Appeals. Such incidents reveal that many police forces need to upgrade their training to include high-stress scenarios, according to respected police training officer Lieutenant Dean T. Olson of the Douglas Country Sheriff's Department in Omaha, Nebraska: "An improper shooting decision carries the potential for costly civil damages, criminal prosecution, strained community relations, and ruined professional and personal lives."

Awareness of Fear Distortions

In life-and-death situations, a person's emergency fear system often creates an altered perception of what is actually going on. The more fear you feel, the narrower your focus becomes as your fight-or-flight response intensifies to help you deal with the immediate threat. In fact, your focus can narrow by 70 percent or more and make it appear as though you are looking down a tunnel or a tube. And if the rising arousal remains unchecked, it can lead to a condition known as hyper-vigilance, in which the person freezes or panics. "Not uncommonly, officers experiencing this might repeatedly pull the trigger of an empty weapon, misidentify innocuous items as weapons or not see or hear innocent bystanders in the line of fire," Olson says.

As well, a police officer, firefighter, soldier, or paramedic may experience other altered perceptions which are geared to help them in a crisis but may hinder seeing the big picture and remembering details of what actually happened:

- Tachypsychia. Events seem to transpire in slow motion and to take longer than they actually do.

- Auditory exclusion, or tunnel hearing. What the brain deems irrelevant is ignored.

- Cognitive dissonance. A series of events may be remembered out of sequence. Trivial happenings may assume exaggerated importance in a person's memory while some major aspects may be blotted out.

- Denial response. An officer may at first deny responsibility for shooting a suspect but admit it afterwards, once his arousal levels return to normal.

- Psychological splitting. A person thinks there are two of him; the passive self stands watching in horror as the active self responds physically to the situation.

- Excorporation. This is the perception of having seen something from outside your own body.

- Amaurosis fugax, or temporary blindness. The mind becomes so terrorized by what it is seeing that it refuses to look at it any more.

- Shock. There is numbness, dulling of the senses, and no awareness of feelings.

These altered perceptions during fight or flight do not occur in every life-and-death situation, but they have been reported often. And they are difficult to reproduce in training, because the emergency services personnel would actually have to be threatened with death in order for their emergency fear system to reach the fight-or-flight stage.

Many emergency services personnel are not even aware of their own reactions to a fearful situation, says Wayne Hill of Chicago, a forensic expert and former police officer and ambulance attendant: "They don't even realize that they are operating on narrow focus and blind adrenaline." Hill recommends that police force themselves to keep their minds flexible and active to see the big picture around them. "If you are a cop, you have to keep assessing your options, where you can duck when you're in a confrontation with a suspect, where you are going to hit him and how you can get him distracted and handcuffed."

According to Bruce K. Siddle, director of PPCT Management Systems, which organizes training sessions in the use of deadly force, officers and soldiers should be taught to develop the habit of moving their head rather than just darting their eyes, to compensate for tunnel vision.

Emergency Dispatcher: Monotone Calm

Unlike many other emergency services personnel, dispatchers do not have the chance to physically discharge the distress which can build up during their hectic days. Although many say they thrive on adrenaline, a calm, neutral disposition is recommended for success. "I have to be monotone calm in a hairy situation," says Richard Schomp, a dispatcher with Sunstar Emergency Medical Services in Pinellas County, Florida. Schomp was named 1994 Dispatcher of the Year by the Florida EMS office for his handling of a forty-three-year-old woman who got chest pains at work and collapsed into cardiac arrest. "None of her coworkers knew CPR, so I taught them over the phone and they did CPR until EMS arrived," he says. The woman recovered.

Dispatchers get into trouble when they let their emotions or ego interfere with their job, says Dr. Jeff Clawson, owner of Medical Priority Consultants Inc. in Salt Lake City, Utah. In 1984 in Dallas, for example, a fire dispatcher argued with a man pleading for an ambulance for his dying mother. "They have to be trained in dealing with stress. We tell dispatchers not to kill the messenger," Clawson says. "Don't beat up the callers if they're upset, because they're really asking for help. Dispatchers have to be fairly unflappable."

"God forbid that you get excited, because if you do you're adding to it," says Joanne Figdore, a medical dispatcher in Boca Raton, Florida.

In a tense rescue situation, it is necessary for one or more personnel to focus on the big picture during a life-and-death struggle, says Deputy Chief Gerald Jones of the Seattle Fire Department. "Stress sometimes causes individuals to focus to potentially dangerous levels with peripheral vision that is too narrow. If the individual is trying to get someone out of an automobile, there is the potential not to notice gasoline coming out of the engine, blowing towards a source of ignition. You should try to have enough personnel around whose responsibility it is to see the entire event, to monitor everyone's safety."

Emergency personnel usually get more effective in such crisis situations the more times they respond to pressure, he adds.

Fear's Physical Impact

Altered perceptions are not the only changes that emergency services personnel must worry about when they become aroused. When their emergency fear system kicks in at medium to high levels, their abilities may be enhanced in some respects (especially fighting, heavy lifting, and running) but may deteriorate in many others (focusing, using equipment such as fire hoses, guns, or chainsaws).

As the heart rate rises, fine and complex motor skills deteriorate quickly as blood is directed away from the fingers and hands to the major muscles (the arms, chest, and thighs). See the sidebar on page 42 for details on the effects of increased heart rates. To help compensate for these physical changes, some police departments are experimenting with the stances their officers take while shooting a gun. (Under heavy duress, an officer's arms and legs may shake, rendering traditional gun-firing methods ineffective.)

Due to the effects of the emergency fear system on motor skills, people required to conduct fine motor-skill tasks (snipers, electronic equipment operators, or drivers) should be protected from direct front-line combat, Bruce Siddle says. "If possible, a unit should also maintain a reserve of individuals who have not been in direct combat and who can be called forward if a precision or fine motor skill is required."

Dynamic Training

Lieutenant Dean Olson recommends what he calls *dynamic training* for police officers: practicing through realistic simulation in order to help officers handle deadly force decisions. This technique employs role-playing scenarios involving live adversaries who act as suspects, and it allows the officers and the suspects to shoot one another with "modified" guns loaded with marking dye. This raises stress levels because the dye not only records the officer's accuracy but strikes with enough force to cause minor bruising.

Also recommended in such training is visualization. In visualization, an officer imagines the potential scenarios of a confrontation, including what weapons she might face and the options that might be available to deal with the situation. She should rehearse as vividly as possible in her mind, "seeing" and "hearing" and "smelling" what might take place in order to both raise stress levels and learn to think at such levels, Olson says. "Visualization reduces reaction time, especially when the officer visualizes more than one option."

Dynamic training should also include tactical breathing—adding more oxygen to control the heart rate, thus reducing anxiety and improving perception. During training, participants' heart rates should be monitored to give feedback about individual stress levels. Olson also recommends that training sessions be videotaped to provide feedback.

Dynamic training is designed to make up for the shortcomings of traditional training methods. The main problem with existing law enforcement training, Olson says, is that "in many cases [it] is conducted in the static, non-threatening, low-stress environment of the gun range, gymnasium or classroom. A common example is traditional firearms qualification on the gun range, in which officers fire only on command at identical paper targets that do not return fire."

Bruce Siddle says one of the more effective ways to simulate warfare is through paintball games, in which participants can be slightly injured. Research shows that when some officers first play the paintball game, their heart rate is well over 200 beats per minute and sometimes up to 300. Through experience, it falls to a range of 115 to 145, which Siddle calls the "optimal survival range," allowing maximum concentration and reaction time.

The Element of Surprise

Most training sessions seldom, if ever, address surprise assault encounters, according to Samuel D. Faulkner, an instructor at the Ohio Peace Officer Training Academy in Columbus, Ohio, and Lieutenant Larry P. Danaher of the Lafayette, Indiana, Police Department, in their report in the FBI Law Enforcement Bulletin. "Today's trainers should strive to teach techniques that better prepare officers to respond to such situations," Faulkner said.

When a person is surprised by a sudden threat, whether it is an armed suspect or a falling object, the fight-or-flight reaction tends to override any training the person has had. The first, natural, and overwhelming reaction is to get away from the threat. Because of this, Faulkner and Danaher say, the best response to teach officers may be a momentary disengagement followed by a controlled re-engagement. Although this may contradict some long-held beliefs, such an approach may be more realistic than expecting a startled officer to immediately control a subject, they add. "Officers should be trained to rely on their own abilities with the aid of equipment, rather than relying on the equipment itself to control resistive subjects," Faulkner said.

Police defensive maneuvers should be based on gross motor skills which use large muscle groups and follow natural patterns, they say, so that the ability of the officer to execute the moves will not deteriorate as arousal levels increase.

Exercise: Controlling Fear and Emotion

Controlling the heart rate is vital when trying to control fear and emotions. It is also the answer to survival performance, Bruce Siddle says. This can be done partly through staying calm, controlling your thought patterns and slowing your breathing. Siddle says you should become aware of a fast heart rate by listening; you can hear it pounding in your chest. He suggests lowering the heart rate by breathing in while counting one, two, three, holding your breath for another one, two, three, then finally breathing out one, two, three. This method, repeated three times, can bring your heart rate down considerably.

My fear formulas also adapt well to survival performance, particularly the alliance of emotions. For situations that are not life-threatening, it seems best to switch your mindset to neutral because you may have to see a big picture and make numerous decisions involving more than one person. But in an encounter with a single suspect or a single threat, the fear-to-anger-to-dispassion response may be the best.

Good Stress

Many police officers and other emergency services personnel have reported that high levels of arousal actually help them perform better than normally, but that this only happens when they manage to apply their nervousness to their work.

Corporal Ron Thompson of the Ontario Provincial Police reported superior concentration in a gun battle with a suspect who was holding Thompson's partner hostage in Woodstock, Ontario, in 1984. He recalled the altered perceptions which helped him to focus: "A gray mantle, like a blanket, was rolled down. Suddenly everything was gone—the street, the traffic, the moon, my partner. All that was left was the gunman and me. His head was transformed into a white oval egg. Very sharp. I shot him between the eyes ... and killed him."

Firefighter Stephen Ruda advises firefighters to stay cool as much as possible to keep their stress hormones under control. "And that helps others keep their cool, as well. True leadership is when those all about you are losing [their] heads and you're keeping yours."

If controlled, the tachypsychia phenomenon can give someone more feedback than normal, allowing better reaction time, Wayne Hill says. "You definitely can make more room in time to make a decision. You start seeing things faster and perceiving them faster. It's like a high-speed movie camera. Each frame is a perception, and you perceive them at a much faster rate." Hill says this condition once helped him control his car as it skidded. "I saw the pavement through the windshield as the car started to nosedive. But I managed to think fast enough to correct the skid."

Police Pursuits

High-speed police chases can bring an officer's emergency fear system (even fight or flight) into play. "It's an enormous rush, an adrenaline rush, extremely exciting and tense and dangerous," says Geoffrey Alpert, a criminology professor at the University of South Carolina and an expert on police pursuits.

During chases, police can go into an emotional fury, says Joseph McNamara, the former police chief in San Jose, California. "They allow their personal anger to get involved, and it's not hard to do."

The difficulty is that there are few ways to release the emotions, says Steve Bunting, executive-director of the American Society of Law Enforcement Trainers in Delaware. "The most you can do is press on the accelerator pedal or a microphone key or squeeze a steering wheel. When you get out of the car, you are basically in a survival mode. People, and police officers are people, have a tendency in this state to act aggressively."

Some police departments have stopped high-speed pursuits and others have modified them.

Controlling the situation under high arousal takes confidence, experience under fearful conditions, and the use of mental cues, Hill adds.

Humor

Humor is a widely accepted technique among emergency services personnel for reducing arousal and maintaining emotional control.

During the Vietnam War, a reconnaissance platoon from the First U.S. Marine Division was depleted to twelve badly wounded men—armed with eight bullets and a few rocks—surrounded by hundreds of North Vietnamese troops on the rocky summit of Hill 488. As dawn loomed in the Que Son Valley, the heavily armed Vietnamese went into a chant in broken English: "Hey, Marines, you die in an hour!"

But then Staff Sergeant Jimmie Earl Howard, wounded so severely he could not move his legs, unleashed his secret weapon: he ordered his men to laugh as loudly as they could from the foxholes of their lonely terrain. This tactic deflated the bravado of the enemy, leading them to believe they must be facing more and healthier Americans than they had anticipated. The tactic also eased the Americans' physical pain and tension and boosted their morale. They were able to hold out until help arrived.

Police use humor all the time. In Calgary, a suspect pulled a knife and a gun on Staff Sergeant Mike Dungey, leaving the officer "scared out of my damn tree." But instead of running for cover like some of his colleagues did or reaching for his revolver, Dungey pulled out another weapon—his humor. "Jeez, George [the suspect's name], you could hurt somebody with those damn things!" Dungey chuckled. "If you shoot me, you'll have to pay for my funeral expenses." For the next thirty minutes, Dungey negotiated with the man before arresting him. "I was joking just as much for me as I was for him," says Dungey, who believes the humor relieved much of his distress and kept him thinking clearly.

> **Strategy Notes for Dealing with Emergencies**
>
> - **Awareness:** Be aware that as heart rate rises, strength and desire improve, but complex motor skills decrease. At high arousal, you may have altered perceptions.
> - **Management:** Train under pressure. See the big picture and keep your mind active. Don't take things personally.
> - **Focus:** Pour your fear energy into the task, or use the alliance of emotions to get out of fear/freeze.

16
The Pressure of Driving

"My philosophy is that sooner or later in life, we must all merge."
—Gary McDonald, a medical practice consultant, on driving

If there is a place where we need a formula to relieve pressure these days, it is on our roads and highways. Researchers say that too many drivers are reporting tension, fear, and even anger behind the wheel—in other words, their emergency fear system is too dominant a force as they drive. These are impaired drivers—impaired not by drugs they ingest but by the powerful drugs already present in their system (adrenaline, testosterone, and dopamine). There should be a separate section in the criminal code for such driving.

And here, in a nutshell, is a technique to make driving not only less distressful and less dangerous but more enjoyable: *shift your mind into neutral.* Too many people are driving with their minds, as well as their bodies, in high gear. For drivers who are nervous and defensive, "neutral" means gearing up a little to a more confident state of mind. For drivers who get irritable and angry, it means gearing down.

When you get behind the wheel of your vehicle, shift your mind into neutral before you even turn the key. Tell yourself that you will not get out of control in traffic, that you will react to situations—and perhaps to other drivers who are aggressive—with calmness, responsibility, and maturity.

In actual fact, to drive effectively, we need a gear—an arousal level—just slightly above neutral, one which will keep us alert to potential problems: curves in the road, potholes, construction, mechanical failures, sudden weather changes, pedestrians and, of course, other drivers. You don't want to be bored or apathetic; that decreases your reaction time.

White Knuckles: Fear Behind the Wheel

Many people find driving pleasurable, an escape from work and society, while others are tense behind the wheel. Some people become so nervous when they are driving that their emergency fear system kicks in, even to levels nearing the fight-or-flight response, according to Dr. Jonathan Abramowitz, clinical director of the Center for Treatment and Study of Anxiety at the University of Pennsylvania School of Medicine. "They start to feel dizzy and tense, like they're having a little chest pain."

Researchers have found that drivers worry most about losing control of the vehicle, driving alone and driving with a critical "back-seat" driver. Dr. Franke P. Deane, a psychologist and researcher at the University of Wollongong in Australia, recommends that people overcome their fear of losing control by taking a defensive driving class. "Treatment might involve training in skid control procedures, driving in icy or wet conditions, or maximizing the use of visual cues for making judgments and improving reaction time."

Some people even develop a phobia of driving, Abramowitz says. "I think there are a bunch of people out there who don't seek treatment because they're embarrassed." It is common—and healthy—to be somewhat fearful in traffic, he adds, "but when fears are excessive and cause impairments in the person's functioning, it's a different story."

There are many reasons to be distressed while driving these days. There are now more vehicles on the road, more accidents, more driving styles, and more cases of road rage than ever before. The fast, stressful lives we lead are often mirrored behind the wheel in our tension, nervousness, and anger. We are also working more and perhaps are more tired on our way home.

"If you asked any truck driver, [he or she] would say poor driving habits and unsafe driving habits are shocking out there right now," says David Bradley, president of the Ontario Trucking Association. "What you see every day in the general driving population is scary. Everyone is in a hurry. There is a general lack of courtesy and common sense. And it's not just aggressive driving; it's speeding and talking on the cell phone with one hand and holding a cup of coffee with another and the newspaper is up on the steering wheel."

Ironically, vehicles are probably safer than ever before; they practically drive themselves. Perhaps that is part of the problem: we take them for granted. In doing so, we often do not pay enough attention to the road and the traffic around us. An increasing number of people are using cell phones while driving; others can be seen eating, drinking, or talking to passengers, their heads bobbing back and forth from the road in front of them.

Many of us have lost the sense of being fully involved in the mechanics of driving and so we give up much of the focus we need. In the old days, when vehicles were more of a novelty, we were probably more smitten with driving; now it's just a way to get from point A to point B. However, we can regain the joy we once had in driving by making more of a commitment to it. Why not enjoy your vehicle as the brilliant machine that it is? Why not read up about it in the book in your glove compartment? Some people report that when they take a rudimentary mechanic's course, their sense of control and enjoyment is enhanced.

Road Rage: Anger Behind the Wheel

If you drive aggressively, chances are your testosterone levels and blood pressure will rise, you will grip the steering wheel tightly, and you may become angry at other drivers. You might even enjoy this mindset; zipping along at seventy miles per hour can be intoxicating. But this state of high arousal can cause problems. "Road rage" has become a catch phrase in our society.

"I really don't understand what happened out there," Circuit Judge Al Crowson said while sentencing forty-one-year-old Shirley Henson to thirteen years in prison for the shooting death of another motorist in Birmingham, Alabama, in 1999. "I look at you and it puzzles me." Court was told that Henson tailgated another female driver for several miles along Interstate 65 as the two women drove home from work, and then a confrontation occurred. Henson said she feared for her life before shooting the other driver, a mother of three.

Robert M. Sapolsky, a neuroscientist and biologist at Stanford University, says that in modern-day society, there is less accountability unless you are dragged into court. "Like our primate relatives, we were designed for living in a group with sixty to one hundred individuals, but we humans now spend most of our lives surrounded by strangers. This gives us a feeling of anonymity, especially when we're inside cars, that frees us to behave like real louts. If a male primate is mean to a female primate, her whole family will come after him. We don't have that sort of accountability in industrial societies."

Getting worked up over a traffic incident can arouse your ego defense and subsequently your emergency fear system to the point where you feel powerful. When the painkiller endorphin is released through the system, it can also deaden any pain you may have been feeling. During a traffic incident in 2000 in Toronto, Brad Root, a job placement counselor, got so worked up that the chronic pain he had been feeling in his back disappeared while he focused on a driver who had cut him off twice. "Suddenly I felt strong and all my pain was gone," he says. When the driver of the other vehicle stopped and got out to talk to Root, they both backed off and the situation ended.

Defusing Fear and Anger

As we have seen throughout this book, we often have the option of defusing our feelings of tension, fear, anger, and arousal or channeling them into the activity. When driving, however, we do not have much choice. If we want to remain safe, we must defuse our emotions.

Let's consider the various techniques we have for reducing high arousal. If we are generally agitated or tense (perhaps after a bad day at the office), there are a number of techniques at our disposal. Driving experts say that listening to your favorite music on radio, tape, or CD can be relaxing. And so our formula for success becomes *fear-to-calmness-to-dispassion*.

Humor is also a good outlet for road tension. Professional speaker and author Allen Klein recalls a woman who was pulled over by a police officer for speeding. She rolled down the window and told him, "Hi, officer. How would you like to buy a ticket to the highway patrolmen's ball?" In the spirit of justice, I must say that this did not help. The officer wrote her a ticket, but he also replied with a joke of his own: "Don't you know, highway patrolmen don't have balls?" Although she still drove off with a ticket, the woman's use of humor helped decrease her stress levels. Humor cannot only put you in a good mood, Klein says, it can also relax your emergency fear system.

The same can be said for music you can sing to, which relaxes your muscles. My wife, Jennifer, who spends two hours each day in a sea of red brake lights to and from downtown Toronto, enjoys singing along with her CDs. Maybe that's why she's usually in a good mood when she gets home.

If our anger is focused on another driver, we need to shift our thoughts away from that driver and concentrate instead on the mechanics of driving. We could do this by briefly putting the emphasis on ourselves: Why are we angry? Do we want to punish the other driver for cutting us off? "When people have wronged us," says Richard Driscoll, a psychologist in Knoxville, Tennessee, "we punish them by being mean so they won't do it again."

Sometimes we need to give a driver who has wronged us the benefit of the doubt, says Matthew McKay, co-director of Haight-Ashbury Psychological Services in San Francisco. "If someone cuts you off, you become offended at his lack of consideration for you and the feeling that you don't count causes you pain, indignation, and resentment. Ire is helpful and necessary in certain cases. It establishes boundaries. If somebody is invading your personal space and therefore you feel threatened, it's anger that helps you keep that person at whatever distance is appropriate. But if you thought the driver must be in a terrible hurry for some good reason, perhaps rushing his sick child to the hospital, you'd have no hard feelings."

Some people take it personally if another driver passes them. Yes, we each have our own territory to protect—and nature provides us with emotional systems as resources against threats—but is the entire road your territory? Aren't we all in that territory? When you become less territorial and less selfish behind the wheel, you will probably relax more.

While the ego defense can be productive in professional and competitive settings, people should put the brakes on ego when they get into a car, says clinical research psychologist Steven L. Fahrion, who recommends shifting quickly back into neutral if you feel yourself getting angry. If you do become angry, the safe alternative may be to talk to yourself rather than race your car ahead to exact revenge. "Sometimes you have to express your feelings," Fahrion says. "Suppressing them can be unhealthy and can begin a kind of vicious cycle that will amplify your anger rather than discharge it."

Most of the time, though, a deep breath and perspective are what is required, according to Dr. Arnold Nerenberg, a clinical psychologist specializing in driving issues. "Take a deep breath and let go," he advises motorists. "Resist the almost irresistible impulse to respond. Do what's necessary to report the driver, but don't invite escalation. Avoid a discussion or anything that could be taken as a hostile reaction, even eye contact." That technique would be *fear-to-letting-go-to-driving*.

Strategy Notes for Driving Safely

- **Awareness:** Understand that you may be tense behind the wheel and that you might allow your ego to be challenged.
- **Management:** Shift your attitude into neutral. Listen to music, but don't allow yourself to be distracted. If you are too tired, consider alternative transportation.
- **Focus:** If a tense situation arises, focus on getting out of it without taking it personally.

The Top 10 Signs You Need to Adjust Your Driving

10. You know what you look like in other people's rear-view mirrors.
 9. You keep touching your St. Christopher medal.
 8. You begin to think that everyone waves with one finger.
 7. The only thing you have calluses from is gripping the steering wheel.
 6. Your insurance rates are going up and your brakes are going down.
 5. Your car radio is picking up static—from you.
 4. Passengers are moving their feet like there are pedals in front of them.
 3. When you pull into the driveway, your passengers kiss the ground.
 2. Your dog doesn't stick its head out the window.
 1. You don't enjoy driving.

If a traffic incident does result in a physical confrontation, it's best to apologize—even if you believe you haven't done anything wrong, Nerenberg says (although you might want to memorize the conversation for possible future use in a police report). His research suggests that 65 percent of road ragers simply want an apology.

Driving can be a pleasure for people if they view it as a chance to get away from stress and competition, says Mihaly Csikszentmihalyi, author of books on the flow experience. "It can give them the most consistent sense of freedom and control; while driving they can concentrate on their problems without interruptions, and resolve emotional conflicts in the protective cocoon of their personal vehicle."

A final note: driving in rush hour can be a great chance to develop your patience, discipline, and ability to cope with problems and distress. Look on your car as a classroom.

17
Everyday Stress and Phobias

"The problem is that many of our weapons are beautifully designed, but for the wrong war. The enemy has greatly changed ... Stresses such as overcrowding, traffic, pollution and government red tape were hardly even in existence until the last couple of centuries."
—Peter G. Hanson, *The Joy of Stress*

Shortly after terrorists slammed airplanes into the World Trade Center and the Pentagon on September 11, 2001, many people commented that they were embarrassed about the things they had fretted over prior to that. "What on earth were the things we worried about before this?" said Bill Mahr, host of the TV show *Politically Incorrect*. "Look at how we've over-reacted to nearly nothing."

Indeed, the horror of that day underscored how often we let small things balloon into large pressures. Sure, there are serious problems to overcome from time to time in your life; but suddenly, the territorial hassle with your neighbor, your daughter's overdue library book, and the frustration of your Internet server crashing were put into their place as minor occurrences which too often set off your emergency fear system.

Sadly, researchers and experts tell us that there is more pressure than ever before in our day-to-day lives, much of it self-imposed. This can result in eustress (good stress), but too often it produces distress (the yucky stuff). Using my three strategies of fear management, we need to become better aware of our stresses. We need to keep pressures at a manageable level and learn to use techniques to change our emotional chemistry when it is counter-productive.

On a big scale, discovering the causes of the stress and pressures in your life can help make them more manageable. If you are continually tense or nervous, it likely means that you are defending yourself. But against what? You may need to examine your attitude, your goals, and even your belief system. Perhaps you shouldn't take things so personally. Perhaps you should lengthen your fuse. Continued distress can cause illness; research shows that 60 to 90 percent of visits to doctors' offices are prompted by conditions related to stress.

But what if the reverse is true? What if you see nothing as a challenge or threat? When you find yourself in need of passion or energy for your day or for a particular job, you can pump yourself up with thoughts of excitement, joy, or even controlled anger. Anger is a good trigger when you are lazy—too lazy to wash up or go volunteering or fix the backyard fence. Tell yourself that this is not acceptable, and then get on with your task. Use your anger as a catalyst for getting into the task, and then let the task take over. Controlled anger is also a good emotion when a wrong needs righting. Perhaps a plumbing company has taken advantage of you and you need to get motivated to call the Better Business Bureau.

Other passionate emotions are good when your life is boring. Dammit, make something of your life! Get yourself excited when dealing with others. Your enthusiasm can rub off and come back to help you, too. Too much stress can kill you, but without enough you're not really living.

Whatever your issues with stress may be, you need a personalized game plan. "No one single idea or technique can magically relieve all your stress, nor does every technique or approach work equally well for everyone," says stress counselor and author Allen Elkin. "You need to put together a package of ideas and methods that you can integrate into the various aspects of your life. It extends from caring about what goes into your mouth to the kind of chair you sit in; from how much sleep you get to how to turn off your racing mind. Effective stress management really comes down to effective lifestyle management."

A variety of emotional techniques can be applied to many stressful situations, from dealing with your children to motivating yourself to do housework to getting a grip when the post office delivers a pile of bills. The decision we must make when we are out of emotional sync is whether to switch our mindset to neutral (or to use one of the two formulas described in Section III: *fear-to-dispassion* or *fear-to-passion-to-dispassion*).

Most situations in everyday life that create pressure or tension can simply be defused by switching your emotions to neutral. Remember that these feelings are almost always the result of your emergency fear system or your worry system. Those systems, particularly the former, have been activated to help you fight, flee, or fake—but most situations today don't require this type of response.

Neutral—a state of calmness or serenity—is a good mindset for many day-to-day tasks because it avoids too many highs and lows. Psychologists say that if we were more neutral about things, there wouldn't be so much distress; they say that most people today have a serious inability to relax. "Most people generally don't know how to rest or relax," says British psychologist Helen Graham. Even if you are approaching an important meeting with your child's teacher or making your first appearance at a private club, neutral is probably a good way to start; you can always change your chemistry as the need arises.

Some Ways of Dealing With High Levels of Stress

- Consult with your physician.
- Relax with meditation, deep breathing.
- Escape (read, watch TV, listen to music, pursue hobbies).
- Exercise.
- Put your life into perspective.

Healthy and Unhealthy Worry

In our efforts to deal with our fears, we can't always react through our worry system. Some fears have to be overcome, some defused, and others redirected.

Healthy fears can be redirected for good purpose. A healthy fear motivates you to improve your weaknesses and work on your skills, to prepare for the threat of opposition or danger. A healthy fear can help us to victory in a tough situation, whether it's in a job, family, or social setting. But it must be a realistic fear, one which you can have some control over. Worrying about a job interview can be a good thing. It may prompt you to review your

Are You Aware That You're Tense?

Sometimes you may not be aware that you are nervous or tense. These feelings don't have to occur during a tough job or situation; just worrying can bring them on. Stop and ask yourself the following questions:

- Are my shoulders slightly raised or hunched?
- Are my muscles slightly tensed?
- Are my teeth clenched?
- Are there knots in my stomach?
- Is my mind racing?
- Am I feeling confrontational?

If you answered yes to any of the above, you may need to relax and let go, or channel the feelings into production. For the big picture, you might want to analyze what has triggered your emergency fear system. Do you really need to defend yourself?

skills and the job description, think through your goals and put your references in place.

Healthy worriers make lists of things that have to be done. John Reed, CEO of Citicorp, begins his day by setting priorities. "I am a great lister. I have twenty lists of things to do all the time. If I ever have five free minutes, I sit and make lists of things that I should be worrying about."

Most fears, however, are unhealthy, psychologists say. "Most fear today is psychological," says author and motivator David J. Schwartz. "Worry, tension, embarrassment, panic, all stem from mismanaged, negative imagination." Unhealthy fears often come from negative programing of the subconscious mind. In general, they must be defused ASAP; otherwise, our hormonal defense weapons will be turned against us as a type of "friendly fire" in the form of anxiety and distress.

The following is a breakdown of the things that most people spend time worrying about:

- Things that never occur: 40 percent of these surveyed
- Things in the past: 30 percent of these surveyed
- Needless concerns about health: 12 percent of these surveyed
- Petty and miscellaneous cares: 10 percent of these surveyed
- Legitimate concerns: 8 percent of these surveyed

"Most of your fears are unjustified," says clinical psychologist Simone Ravicz, an adjunct professor at Saybrook Graduate School in northern

California. "I call this 'stinking thinking.' This magnifies the bad and ignores the good, as in 'Nothing I do matters' or 'I'm late with the rent and I'll be evicted' or 'Everyone will be watching when I speak and I'll probably make a fool of myself.'" Ravicz suggests that people keep a journal of these negative thoughts.

Some people even "catastrophize," according to Paul G. Stoltz, a consultant for many top U.S. corporations. "People catastrophize when they turn everyday inconveniences into major setbacks and those setbacks into disasters," he says. "Catastrophizing often involves destructive rumination over bad events. The more one mulls the event over in one's mind, the more ominous it becomes and the more serious and likely the consequences appear ... You don't have to experience a nervous breakdown to feel drained and anxious."

Unhealthy fears usually fit into two groups:

1. An unrealistic fear of something that will probably never happen, or fear of things beyond your control. Examples: Fear of an airplane crashing; of walking the streets at night, even though the crime rate is low; of what downtown traffic will be like when it's time to drive home; of how your child will do in a performance.
2. Dwelling on a realistic fear so much that you exaggerate it or feel the pain several times over.

Unhealthy fears can be reduced by thinking things through logically or by research. For example, if you have a fear of flying, read up on the statistics which show that it's the safest way to travel, or talk to friends who fly a lot. Sharing your worries with others can also put them in perspective. Some people call this *connecting*.

Phobias

If you are unusually anxious about a particular situation, you may have a phobia. A phobia is a morbid, unrealistic fear that causes people to avoid situations or things. In a mild form, a phobia might cause a person to avoid a

Exercise: Worry Busters

When you feel worried or anxious about an upcoming situation, take the following steps:

- Recognize the worry as a fear and identify where it comes from. It may be fear of failure or fear of what others think.
- Separate healthy fears from unhealthy fears.
- Try changing your mindset: most unhealthy fears must be defused as soon as possible.
- Redirect your healthy fears into preparation or action.
- Recognize that you have control. In general terms, life is probably 20 percent what happens to you and 80 percent how you react.
- Concentrate on the solution, not the problem.
- If worries persist, share them with others.

---

certain route to work in the morning; in a more serious form, it could keep that person home altogether or lead to panic attacks.

There are basically three types of phobias: phobias of specific objects or situations (such as spiders, heights, or flying); social phobias, in which a person fears embarrassment or humiliation; and agoraphobia, the fear of being away from a safe place. At their worst, these phobias can turn your emergency fear system and worry system into punishing mechanisms which can make you ill.

Phobias are pretty common. In my immediate family of about thirty people, I've discovered fears of fainting, baths, spiders, boredom, people, escalators, flying, and not being able to control a televised hockey game (my uncle used to move articles around on a coffee table to influence the outcome). The most common phobias are fear of public speaking, of flying, and of going to the dentist. It's estimated that one out of ten people has a serious phobia, and most people suffer in silence.

Sometimes there is no explanation for how a phobia develops, but in many cases it begins with a traumatic event—such as waking up to find a hairy spider on your forehead and discovering that you've been bitten. Some people shrug off these incidents while others are haunted by them for years. Some psychologists believe the root of phobias lies in a combination of genetic predisposition, environment and social causes.

Phobias carry a big price tag. Fear of flying costs people promotions, relationships, nice holidays, even their jobs, and it costs the U.S. air travel industry well over $1 billion a year in potential revenue (even before the terrorism of September 2001). "I've seen people turn down job promotions because it involved getting on a plane," says Tracy Summer, a clinical social worker, "and a number of older women who missed a relative's wedding." She also counseled a young woman who stopped seeing a man who wanted her to fly with him on business trips. It's estimated that twenty-five million Americans are afraid of flying. The fear usually surfaces at about age twenty-seven, and women are twice as likely to suffer from it than men. As with many other phobias, sufferers experience shallow or rapid breathing, heart palpitations, trembling, sweaty palms, dizziness, feelings of terror and, in extreme cases, hysteria.

"I stopped flying because of panic attacks," says Warren Elkins, a computer consultant for a major insurance company. When faced with the possibility of flying, Elkins would break out in cold sweats, fearful he would faint. "I was never in a crash [and] didn't even have a bad experience. It just happened." On a routine flight from Dallas to San Francisco, Xerox executive William Ernisse suffered nausea and chest pains and had to be treated by paramedics. "It scared the living daylights of out me," he says.

Mental health experts say that people don't fear flying as much as they do relinquishing control. Victims are often worriers or perfectionists. "They tend to be imaginative, creative, intelligent, excitable, and emotional," says Julian Herskowitz, a psychologist in Huntington, New York. "They also tend to be people who are likeable, pleasant, and personable. They have a good sense of humor. They are not people we would think of as having something wrong with them."

"It's difficult giving up control," says actor Joaquin Phoenix. "It just scares me. These dudes are in the cockpit, but you can't get to know them, and it's like 'Man, you have my life!'"

Perhaps fear of flying is so common because it encompasses a number of other fears: fear of heights, fear of closed-in places and fear of death. Surveys show only 38 percent of "aviaphobes" fear crashing. They worry more about the loss of control, of embarrassing themselves, or fainting.

Phobias often run in families, says Laszlo Papp, director of the Anxiety Disorders Research Program at Long Island Jewish Medical Center. "We know these people breathe differently. You can look at brain imaging scans and you can see different things trigger different mechanisms. There's definitely a biology to this. We are looking at these people and trying to get closer to the cause."

Depending on the severity of a phobia, sufferers may want to expose themselves to their fear in order to overcome it. Since many phobias are programed through experience, imagination, or instruction, they can also be deprogramed. Sometimes imagining or visualizing the experience can help.

I don't know how I got my fear of dentists, doctors, and gory movies, which has caused me to pass out from time to time. But I do know that I developed an additional fear from those experiences—of fainting. At times, this fear has led to my teeth and health being neglected. I've been able to reduce those fears by about 70 percent through "exposure." A dramatic improvement was made when I volunteered to be a victim for a mock automobile accident staged by the fire department. They put me in a smashed-up car and painted me up like I was on the verge of death—and I felt that way, too. However, I had no choice but to behave and force my way through the situation: the whole episode was being taped for the six o'clock news!

Strategy Notes for Decreasing Worry

- **Awareness:** Be aware that most of your worries are probably out of perspective, causing you distress.
- **Management:** Balance your life physically, professionally, socially, and spiritually.
- **Focus:** For the important issues, don't get uncontrolled anger, get results.

For serious phobias, prescription drugs (such as benzodiazepine) or the help of a professional therapist may be needed.

For more information on phobias and anxiety, contact 1-888-ANXIETY (269-4389). Operated by the National Institute of Mental Health, this service offers pamphlets and a list of resources.

V
Harnessing Fear's Physical Gifts

This section looks at the type of situations our emergency fear system was originally designed for: physical crises and confrontations. It would be fairly easy to adapt our natural arousal defenses to meet such challenges, but in our safe society we don't get much experience in fighting or fleeing.

Chapter 18 will focus on how to deal with your reaction to a fearful circumstance and get your arousal hormones under control. Included is a natural technique that has been too often neglected: surviving for the sake of loved ones, or at least thinking about them while in trouble. Chapter 19 examines emotional methods for surviving an attack by an assailant. In Chapter 20, we will learn how to become more effective rescuers.

18
The Enemy Within: Dealing With Your Own Reaction

"I must stay in control."
—rape victim Charlene Smith

The first person you must control in a physical confrontation or crisis is you. Tom Burnett obviously knew this. He was a passenger on United Airlines flight 93, hijacked by terrorists on that dark Tuesday of September 11, 2001.

With panic all around him, Burnett telephoned his wife Deena in their California home. Rather than crying and telling his family how much he loved them, as some other passengers did, Burnett used his four phone calls to exchange information in an attempt to prevent the jet from crashing into the White House.

"In the first call, he gave me a few details and told me to call the authorities," Deena recalls. "He was not calling to say good-bye. He was taking down information, he was planning what (the passengers) were going to do. And he was not interested in reviewing his life. He was problem solving and he was going to take care of it."

When Tom realized that other planes had crashed into the World Trade Center in New York and the Pentagon in Washington, he and at least three other passengers decided to rush the knife-wielding hijackers. "He was pumping me for information," Deena said. "His adrenaline was flowing, and he was trying to sort it all out. I think he realized much sooner than I did that it was a suicide mission."

The subsequent actions of Burnett and other passengers—which sparked a wild struggle heard on the cockpit voice recorder—thwarted the hijackers' plans. The plane crashed in the Pennsylvania countryside, killing all on board; but perhaps thousands of American lives were saved by Burnett's controlled focus under high pressure.

As Tom Burnett's case illustrates, controlling yourself in a physical crisis doesn't mean you have to be passive; you can even act with a type of controlled anger or passion. But when you react to an accident, assault, or rescue situation, sudden changes to your mind-body chemistry—and to your whole physiology—make it imperative that you establish control of the new, altered you. Controlling yourself and your emergency fear system is as important as the other major issue: controlling the emergency situation.

Many people cannot function effectively during a crisis, when their arousal system reaches such high levels that it feels like their heart is coming up through their throat. For many people, it is the first (and perhaps only) time in their lives they will feel this level of arousal. We are not used to terrible things happening, and so we are not used to the dramatic physiological response that is generated when they do.

Some people panic even in mock training sessions. Vicki White, an administrative assistant at Arkansas State University, was taking a self-defense class when a mock attacker came up behind her to test her. She froze. "I always thought I was an independent person, but when you have somebody coming after you, I was surprised how I froze up."

Even trained police officers sometimes freeze when confronted with a life-or-death threat. That happened to Debbie Gardner, who was more than halfway through her three-year program at the police academy and at the top of her class, destined to become one of the first women police officers to take up single patrol duty. One night she was assaulted and couldn't defend herself. "I froze," she recalls. "Despite being horribly over-trained, I was a failure. It was a disaster. I hit the wall between what's out on the street and what's in here," she says, patting her heart.

During the assault, Gardner became too emotional—her emergency fear system kicked into overdrive and she could not control it. Her heart raced, her muscles tightened, and she froze on the spot, mentally and physically. "The emotion of the moment is the mountain you have to climb," says

Gardner, now the executive-director of the Survive Institute in Cincinnati, which provides personal protection seminars for companies and self-defense classes for individuals. "In self-defense, the physical part is minimal. Two-thirds has to do with your own emotional reaction to the threat. But if you can control yourself and concentrate your extra strength, then even the wimpiest person can become a powerful animal."

Gardner and other experts believe that most people react to a physical crisis by going into panic or near-panic, or at least get so aroused that they cannot deal with the situation productively. That happens for two reasons: we may be startled by the emergency, and in our society we are not used to physical confrontations. We are more likely to deal effectively with a potential car crash than with an attacker because we are used to controlling our cars mechanically and operating them under stressful conditions of heavy traffic and impatient drivers.

Too often, our fear reaction gets caught in the freeze response. As you will recall, there are four general ways in which we are programed to deal with a serious threat: fighting, fleeing, faking a fight, or freezing. The freeze mode can be helpful if it allows us a brief time to decide what we are going to do next (perhaps fight, flee, or fake?). But the danger with too much freeze is that it can solidify into panic if we are not careful and do not mobilize ourselves.

These days, most people react to physical crisis negatively and do not mobilize themselves, Gardner says. According to her, these are five common reactions:

- You become short of oxygen and have trouble breathing. "You may not be able to holler for help."
- Your heart starts pounding and its sound can add to your fears. You become afraid of your own fear reaction.
- Your hands and fine motor skills lose their effectiveness as blood is pumped into the major muscles, such as the upper arms and legs.
- Your limbs start to shake. "It's no coincidence that our communities have 911 as the dialing number for emergencies ... the dexterity of your fingertips is reduced. We try to make it as easy as possible for people to dial for help."
- You can't run. "You feel like you're stuck in quicksand or you move in slow motion."

Releasing Yourself from the Freeze Mode

Most people do not know how to breathe properly under stress, never mind in the face of a physical threat, says psychologist Gay Hendricks, former professor at the University of Colorado at Colorado Springs and author of *Conscious Breathing*, a book on breathing techniques. In a crisis, some people start to hyperventilate, taking in such limited amounts of air that they feel faint or even pass out. Forcing yourself to breathe can mobilize your forces. Debbie Gardner says, "I have three words of advice for victims: 'Breathe, breathe, breathe.'" In her seminars she says the word *breathe* "maybe 2,000 times. Because when people freeze, what they're really doing is holding their breath. Air is sucked [in] and trapped in your stomach in large amounts. It's like an emotional punch in the gut. You've got to breathe deeply from your stomach." When some people try this method, it sounds like a scream. But Gardner advises people to grunt with a sound like *ah—oooh!*

Taking deep breaths was one of the keys to success for Roland Sparks, who saved two people's lives in separate accidents, in British Columbia in 1965 and Alberta in 1985. "There was fear," recalls Sparks, an oil company supervisor. "But my first aid training and taking deep breaths got me through."

Another technique for overcoming your fear reaction, Gardner says, is to pump your hand in and out of a fist, squeezing, then letting go. This pulls the blood back into your hands and improves your fine motor skills. "You should keep making your hand into a tight fist, then releasing, two or three times or more. Until you do that, you won't be able to do simple things like getting your key in your door because your motor skills are gone and you shake ... Watch baseball players in the ninth inning. The pitcher takes a deep breath from his stomach and the batter pumps his bat and grips it. Golfers do the same thing."

Another trick for mobilizing yourself, Gardner says, is a type of power talk. "Talk out loud to yourself in strong, positive tones. Most people are loaded with negative talk."

Some people have reported success by using the two-stage fear formula:

the *fear-to-dispassion* response. They are able to shut down thoughts of their own fear reaction by focusing intently on what it takes to get out of the situation.

Truck driver Gordon Rasmussen was so concerned about two men drowning in the Bow River in Calgary in 1981 that he focused all his attention on the victims. The fast-moving water, which had created an undertow, was up to his shoulders, but Rasmussen focused so much on the victims that he forgot he could not swim. "I didn't think—it all happened so fast, I did it on impulse," he said after pulling the men to safety.

Once you are in emotional control of yourself, you will find that you have extra powers, Gardner says. "You become comfortable with that feeling and you suddenly realize you have the power, the physical and mental power, to get out of a traumatic event. You can do it. You can get out of any situation. Yes, untrained people can survive."

The Power of Love

An excellent way to get through a physical crisis is to think of a loved one. In fact, there is some evidence to suggest that this may be a natural response. Over the years, I have interviewed hundreds of victims of accidents, muggings, and other calamities who said they survived because they thought of a close relative or a friend while in the midst of the situation.

Many who were in life-or-death straits reported a sort of life flashback, in which pictures of their loved ones flashed through their mind. I have a theory that this is nature's way of motivating us to get through terrible circumstances. A number of experts, including Canadian neuroscientist Michael Persinger, agree. "When someone is in a threatening situation, they say their life passed before their eyes," Persinger says. He adds that nature knows such a vision will activate a person's emergency fear system, even fight or flight, to try to overcome the danger. "This sets off all kinds of chemical and electrical changes in the brain. Certainly, there is survival value to this, whether it's physical survival or survival professionally or of the ego."

Paul Taenzer, a clinical psychologist at the University of Calgary, had a life flashback when he was injured in a motorcycle accident in Montreal. "It was phenomenal. It happened years ago and the details have been lost to me now, but I saw it all in a few seconds ... life events flashing before my eyes."

August L. Reader, director of the electrophysiology laboratory at the Cedars-Sinai Medical Center and a neuroophthalmologist in Los Angeles, had what he described as a part-flashback, part-near-death experience after his heart stopped in the middle of the night. At first he panicked when his heart wouldn't start beating again, and he feared he was about to die. When he let go, "releasing myself into the arms of God," a sudden calm came over him. "There was a panorama surrounding me, 360 degrees ... of three-dimensional Technicolor, holographic flashes of everything that had occurred in my life, from the most trivial detail to the most important events ... this vision lasted only half a second, then I opened up into this huge expanse of silvery-white light that was inhabited by a multitude of egg-shaped, silvery, crystalline beings with cameo-like faces that were slowly bobbing and bouncing each other. As I looked, I realized the faces, although not perfectly clear, were recognizable as everyone I had known, both alive and dead." Reader believes such experiences are closely related to the fight-or-flight response and he calls near-death "the ultimate reflex of fight or flight, a fear response" partly created by the potent natural painkiller endorphin.

However, when faced with injury or death, we cannot wait and hope for this flashback to save us. We may have to force ourselves to think of loved ones. "You have to think about your children, your wife and your family, to keep you going," says Florida resident Lew Lipsit, who used those thoughts to survive forty-four hours after his boat sank in the stormy waters of the Gulf of Mexico in 2001 (he used his false teeth to catch rain water to drink). "I had to keep going for my family; I knew they'd be sick with worry."

Many athletes use this technique when confronted with an important play or shot. In the 1996 Summer Olympics, Gary Hall Jr., swimming for his grandfather, whom he believed had been falsely imprisoned, won the gold medal for the United States 400-meter medley relay team with a record last lap. In the National Basketball Association, Mark Jackson of the New York Knicks ties his wedding ring into his sneakers so he can look down at it when he needs comforting or motivating.

Thinking of loved ones is most powerful when the situation is critical. In Victoria, British Columbia, in 1989, firefighter Mike Crawford was drowning while scuba diving with a friend. Both his lungs collapsed and air went into his bloodstream and his brain. "I was about as close as you could come to being dead," he recalls. "I wanted to tell my partner to 'Give my love to Leslie' [Crawford's wife], and suddenly I felt calm and relaxed." Rescuers pulled him out and he eventually recovered. "I'm sure thinking of Leslie helped me. She's kind of a fighter. Her attitude always rubs off on me."

Before he became a wrestler and then governor of Minnesota, Jesse Ventura was in the Navy SEALs. He recalls how he nearly died when he fell over the wall of a dam into churning white water: "I was like a pebble in a washing machine, getting sucked down. I accepted the idea I was going to die, but suddenly I started feeling sorry for my mom and dad. I had a very clear vision of the two of them bending over my casket, crying. Then suddenly my feet scraped the river bottom and I shot to the surface."

> ### Doing It for Them
>
> In 1951, Winnie Roach-Leuszler was attempting to become the first Canadian to swim the English Channel. Just 35 feet from the cliffs of Dover, she had a stroke of bad luck when the tide suddenly changed and swept her 5 miles back towards France. Cold, tired and suffering from a jellyfish sting to the face, Winnie got a pep talk from her father, Eddie, who was traveling alongside her in a row boat. Eddie reminded the exhausted and faltering Winnie of her three young daughters back in Toronto. "Hurry, Winnie, hurry!" he shouted. "They want their ice-cream." Suddenly, the energy and the resolve returned to her stroke. "I'd been fading away," she recalled years later, "but the thought of my daughters gave me strength." She completed the ordeal and returned home to a ticker-tape parade in Toronto.

In Hortonville, Wisconsin, in 1993, Lance Meyer was under a 1974 Camaro, fixing it, when the jack fell and the vehicle landed on his face, smashing his glasses and trapping him. "I thought about my girlfriend and I knew I had no choice but to get out of there." Somehow, the skinny, 145-pound Meyer lifted the low-riding vehicle enough to wiggle free. "I guess it was a miracle; there was blood all over the place and I don't know where I got the strength and concentration."

Wayne Hill, a forensic expert and a former police officer and ambulance attendant, once rescued a woman from a car crash by imagining she was his wife. "Hell, at 5-8, 190, I summoned enough power to jump over a 5-foot fence on the dead run to rescue her. In those times, you can make fear your ally."

A catchy phrase for this technique would be *fear-to-loved-ones-to-focus*. And don't forget that third element. Without tight focus on the task, all the motivation in the world isn't good enough, says San Diego police officer Sanford Strong, who teaches officers and SWAT teams how to defend themselves. "You've got to concentrate on the act, whether it's fighting or escaping. The supposed life-flashing-before-my-eyes phenomenon really does happen, but under extreme duress, the mind tends to float about loved ones or family." In the end, Strong says, "you must concentrate on what you have to do to survive."

Exercise: Overcoming a Negative Reaction to High Arousal

- Acknowledge that your emergency fear system is there to help you overcome a crisis.
- Force yourself to breathe deeply, using the stomach.
- Change the emotion of fear briefly to a more passionate emotion, perhaps anger or excitement, then put the energy into the task at hand.
- Talk aloud, reminding yourself that you can do it, that you have powerful resources at your command.
- Think of loved ones, about getting home to them.
- To better manage your emotional pressure, take a course in self-defense.

19
Surviving an Assault

"When fighting for your life, become totally ferocious and ruthless. Become part animal, part machine, a cross between the Terminator and an enraged lion."
—Police training officer Sanford Strong

When faced with an attacker, whether it is a robber, mugger, or rapist, you have more resources to get you through the situation than you think—and more options.

In such circumstances the power of your emergency fear system is usually jacked up to maximum on the arousal meter, or close to it. If you have ever been confronted by an attacker, you might remember the knots in your stomach or how wide your eyes opened. Those sensations testify to the inner resources you possess to deal with such a shocking situation, even if you are not trained. It is up to you to decide whether to mobilize the forces through a passionate response or switch to neutral and try to ease your way out of it.

Your emergency fear system is equipped with at least four natural responses to an attack:

- You can fight.
- You can flee.
- You can freeze.
- You can fake a fight.

Success has been reported by victims using all four of the above responses.

Even while you are supposedly incapacitated by an assailant, your resources can keep you alive. For example, on August 1, 1998, thirty-three-year-old Gina Jourdan was on her way home from work in Springdale, Ohio, when she was accosted by two would-be robbers. One put a gun to her head and the other encouraged him to shoot. Jourdan recalls what she said to the gunman: "I looked at the guy who had the gun to my head and said, 'What the [expletive] do you want?'" The surprised assailant backed off and the two men fled. "I think the vulgar language and my confidence threw him off guard. He'd had all the power in the situation and suddenly he got frustrated."

Jourdan's response is a classic example of the "fake" mode—becoming so arrogant as to think you can ward off an attacker, even one armed with a weapon. It is not the response that some self-defense experts recommend, and yet they admit that it is hard to judge how anyone will react when confronted with such a surprising situation. Every situation is unique and may require a different response from the victim.

If you decide to mobilize your forces for fighting or fleeing (or even faking), my fear formulas can work well. If you are frozen by fear and in a near-panic mode, changing the debilitating fear to anger or passion will get you moving rapidly, giving you more power and speed than you thought you had. Then, of course, you must direct the energy into your physical response, whether it is to fight or to take off fast.

Anger is a nifty trigger, but simply screaming or shouting can also change your emotional chemistry from fear to excitement. "Screaming gets your adrenaline going, helps you to concentrate and prepares you for action," says police officer Sanford Strong. "Screaming may also unsettle your attacker and attract the attention of others. But make it a lion's roar, a battle cry!"

"If you make a run for it, begin with a loud aggressive yelp of 'Fire!'" says Novalee Coates-Drover, a sexual harassment officer. "A yell can intimidate the offender, build your confidence, and improve your strength. Anger is another energizing response. It keeps people thinking and acting. Fear is a paralyzing response. Your best defense is your own intelligence; if you panic, you will be confused and not able to think."

Whenever possible, according to Strong, Coates-Drover and many other experts, you should avoid a fight, especially if it is just over your money or other property. "Avoiding a fight is always the best strategy," says Tanya K. Metaksa, executive director for the National Rifle Association's Institute for Legislative Action and author of a self-defense book, *Safe, Not Sorry*. "Most law-abiding citizens, especially women, have very little fighting experience

... the grim reality is that if you are forced to physically defend yourself against an attacker, even if you survive, you are very likely to be hurt." It is a given that an attacker usually has the upper hand, not only by surprising you but by being prepared. Assailants are often street- or jail-toughened fighters, and they may have picked you out as a vulnerable target.

Perhaps your first response to such a crisis should be to switch your emotions to neutral. This will buy some time to weigh your options and make a decision whether to fight, flee, or fake. You need to keep your mind active and see the big picture, with all its options. Neutral is the opposite of the high-stress mode of blind adrenaline, which you might eventually need for fight or flight. Your reaction to a crisis might automatically shift into a neutral mode if you freeze and stop breathing for a second, as many animals do when confronted by a more dangerous enemy. But if you stay in the freeze mode for too long, it could turn to panic and cement your feet to the ground.

As the confrontation progresses, you may want to switch tactics, as Stacy Rinker, a thirty-three-year-old human resources administrator, did in New York when she and her husband were assaulted by an armed mugger who may have been on drugs. "He came up behind me and grabbed me in a choke hold. I instinctively began fighting, but when I realized he had a knife pressed to my neck, I changed tactics." After the couple determined that the man wanted money, they tossed their cash on the ground. The mugger took it and ran away.

In most instances, Metaksa advises victims to run, run, run. "Run as fast as you can, scream, use a cellular phone, or find someone you can trust to help you." If you have no choice but to fight, remember that your powerful defense system has put extra weapons at your disposal—potent hormones that provide enhanced strength, speed, and concentration when you are in extreme distress. You will have more powers than if you were wrestling with your nephew on the living-room floor. This is your emergency fear system at its natural best. This is what it was designed for millions of years ago, in a harsher world where physical altercations were a part of everyday life.

If it comes down to a fight, experts say you should try to inflict pain upon the attacker—by a kick in the groin, a gouge to the eyes, or a stomp on the foot. Your head is hard, and you can use it to pop the assailant under the jaw. "Criminals don't want to get hurt, either," says Metaksa, who advises victims to use any weapons at their disposal, including fists, feet, elbows, fingernails, and teeth. "As in nature, injured predators become prey themselves. It may buy you a couple of precious seconds." Strong says, "Never fight fair. Your primary target is the eyes, then the throat."

As soon as your physical response buys you some time, *get out of there*. "Inflict pain, deter the attack, and then escape!" Metaksa says. "You stay alive by keeping the fight short and by escaping as quickly as possible." When fleeing, concentrate as much on your form as you do on the person pursuing you, pumping your knees high.

Training

While it is difficult to prepare for random violence, a little training in the fundamentals of fighting or defense cannot hurt. Check the newspapers for courses in your area.

Two weeks before she was attacked, Gina Jourdan had taken a self-defense seminar conducted by Debbie and Mike Gardner at the Survival Institute in Cincinnati. The course outlined steps you can take to escape an attacker, including the option which Jourdan used. A confident victim can sometimes ward off such an offense with words. "Self-defense is rooted in self-esteem," Gardner says. "You've got to learn to control yourself before you can control someone else." Says Jourdan, "It's all about confidence and saying to yourself, 'You are not going to do this to me, and if something does happen, I can deal with it.'"

Stacy Rinker also credits a self-defense class with helping her survive her ordeal. "Everything I did was calculated. I had a sense of control that I would not have had without the training. Because we were calm and in control, we defused what could have been a very bad situation."

Metaksa recommends martial arts geared toward self-defense, especially aikido, aikijutsu, or judo, where grappling moves are taught. "Most street fights end up with the combatants wrestling on the ground. So, grappling skills can save your bacon."

Angela Klit said her training in the obscure martial art hapkido as a child controlled her fight-or-flight reaction when she was beaten and threatened with a knife by two men in Chilliwack, British Columbia, in 2000. "I was in a situation of life and death. It's so weird, the power that comes over you when you're in a situation like that," she said after kneeing one attacker in the groin and kicking the other in the temple.

Let's take a closer look at some real-life examples of the four natural responses to an assault.

Response #1: Fight

Perhaps at one time the "fight" in fight or flight was more prominent than it is today because primitive people had to physically protect themselves against rival bands. Today, for a variety of reasons, few victims fight back. Fighting an attacker, particularly one armed with a weapon, can be hazardous, and police usually discourage it. But fighting has produced results for some people. The owner of a St. Louis, Missouri, gasoline station said he had no choice but to fight off an armed attacker on October 13, 1995.

The owner, who does not want to be identified, said a man walked into his station with a .22-caliber rifle and calmly announced that it was a stick-up. "Then he started losing it. He kept yelling, 'I'm getting antsy, I'm getting antsy.'" The owner, who had a twelve-year-old son, pleaded for his life. "Please don't shoot me. I've got a family." After the owner handed over $200, the man ordered him to kneel down. "That's when I knew he was going to kill me," the victim says.

When the owner reached under the counter for a pistol, the gunman pressed the barrel of the rifle against his head. "I remember thinking 'I'll be damned if I'm going to let him kill me kneeling down without a fight,' so I just grabbed the rifle barrel."

As the pair struggled over the rifle, the robber pulled the trigger and a bullet smashed a nearby lottery machine. The robber then fled the station, but the owner was filled with anger and decided to pursue him with his pistol. "It was the fear and the adrenaline taking over," he says.

He jumped over the counter, but perhaps impaired by an overflow of adrenaline, lost his balance. "That guy's lucky I fell because I would've killed him. I would have shot him in the back and not thought twice about it."

The following day, as police looked for the suspect and a surveillance video of the robbery appeared on local television stations, customers stopped to congratulate the owner. "That's nice, but I was just trying to stay alive," he says, discouraging anyone from believing he was a hero. "Believe me, I'm no Rambo."

Response #2: Flee

Don't underestimate your speed when the devil is pursuing you. On February 24, 1989, Peter Oudman, a blond, bespectacled man who resembles the late singer John Denver, was walking to work at a gas company. Without warning, a crazed man came up behind him with two steak knives and stabbed him in the back. There was no pain at first, but Oudman felt a trickle of hot blood under his shirt. Frightened, he broke into a sprint, with the younger attacker on his tail.

The speed of the fifty-one-year-old Oudman was incredible, especially considering the three-inch-deep knife wound in his back and that he was wearing dress shoes. When he reached his office, Oudman calmly told a receptionist to call the police. She didn't believe he'd been stabbed until he showed her the hole in his trenchcoat.

When the assailant followed him into the building, Oudman ran up the stairs with what he later termed "amazing energy and power," leaping four steps at a time to the second floor. "Part of me was confused why he was doing this because I'd never seen the guy before," Oudman says. "But my concentration was mainly focused on getting away from him."

The suspect's focus was totally on Oudman and he ignored other employees in the office as he chased Oudman throughout the complex. Ironically, Oudman ducked into a room full of workers taking their final exams in a St. John's ambulance first-aid course. Instead of collapsing, Oudman cracked, "Do you want a real patient to practice on?" They dropped their bandages, notepads, and jaws to gawk at the blood on his coat.

"At first, I thought it was part of a scenario, that we were being tested for what we'd learned," says Lou Robichaud, one of the workers. "But then I checked Peter. It was hard to believe he was so calm and in no pain."

Outside the training room, the suspect encountered a police officer. He stabbed the officer three times, but the officer shot him to death.

In retrospect, Oudman believes that his above-average foot speed that day had something to do with his survival instincts. "I was running like hell. I've never run so fast in my life." His friends and family also credit his easy-going nature, his training years before in the Dutch military, and his sense of humor with helping him through the crisis.

Response #3: Freeze

There is still a lot we don't know about the freeze response. It may be related to panic or going into shock, but there seems to be a benefit to freezing in that it gives a victim a chance to weigh a situation, to notice possible exit routes, and to assess the vulnerabilities of a suspect. In the animal kingdom, when a prey believes it cannot fight or outrun a predator, it freezes on the spot, partly to make itself less conspicuous to the predator, but also to buy time for optional responses.

TV personality Maureen O'Boyle, who hosted the popular syndicated show *A Current Affair* in the 1990s, used her freeze mode to gain valuable information about a man who raped her. It happened on April 3, 1986, in Macon, Georgia, where O'Boyle anchored the CBS affiliate's early morning news. Late at night, a man broke into her garden-level apartment, held her hostage for three hours, and raped her. "He was on top of me, threatening me with a knife," O'Boyle recalls. "He told me he was going to hurt me, to kill me, to cut me up."

O'Boyle was gripped with fear. "He terrorized me, put a pillowcase over my head. I felt so weak. It's like gravity is holding you down, and you can't even lift your arm. I've talked to other rape victims who get adrenaline beyond belief, but for me, it was really the opposite. I was paralyzed by my fear."

And yet that fear made her mind sharper. "My brain started working overtime. It was like a tape recorder and a video recorder were running in my mind. I thought, 'I have to remember everything in order to catch him.' And I really knew I was going to survive it. There was no way it was going to end then."

Her sharpened concentration also helped O'Boyle get the assailant out of her apartment. She developed a conversation with him, at times suggesting he would get off scot-free if he left her alone, at other times telling him that her colleagues from work would be checking on her. "I told him if he left now, they wouldn't catch him."

Although he kept her blindfolded or turned to the wall for most of the three hours, O'Boyle managed to get a description of his hands ("He had mechanic's hands, callused, with oil embedded in them"), of his long, blond hair ("I felt it on my neck") and of his voice ("He talked in a very thick, southern accent").

After she had convinced him to leave, O'Boyle caught a glimpse of his white truck. As soon as her ordeal was over and she had called 911, shock kicked in and O'Boyle fainted. But her descriptions helped police to catch the suspect one month later.

While it may have seemed as though O'Boyle was stuck in a freeze, she survived by keeping her mind active in a sort of neutral mode, in which it could keep providing her with valuable information.

Response #4: Fake

In the spring of 1997, I pulled off an all-star fake in Miami. It was nothing to laugh about at the time, though. While jogging outside a reputable hotel in Key Biscayne, I was accosted by a punk about eighteen years old and more muscular than me.

He yelled at me from across the street in threatening tones, then started walking aggressively across toward me. "Hey, get over in the park!" he ordered. I slowed down to look at him and felt afraid, eventually coming to a stop. There was no one around except the two of us and a younger teenager, maybe fifteen. I don't remember his exact words, but the eighteen-year-old ordered me to get down on my knees and put my hands on my head. It sounded as though he'd been watching too many action movies, but for a split second he had me in his control. I could see myself dropping to my knees—but then I imagined him taking my watch and a bracelet my wife, Jennifer, had just given me. That thought seemed to trigger a less passive response. Instead of assuming the police suspect position, I took a wide, confident stance and pointed my finger firmly at him.

"Get back!" I shouted. I couldn't believe those words had come out of my mouth, and in such an impressive fashion. I went from being scared to being angry. In that stance I felt strong and assertive. (It was something I'd seen on a TV documentary about how to dissuade a snarling dog.)

With the assailant still about twenty feet away, I felt as though I had some control, although my next option was to sprint toward the hotel. But my sudden bravado seemed to stop him in his tracks, right in the middle of the street. My second salvo was, "Don't EVER approach somebody like that again!"

Thankfully, he started backpedaling. "Yeah, all right, but remember, I know where you live," he snapped, looking back at his friend. "You're not safe."

Confident now, I walked back to the hotel like a military man, arms swinging, hoping I wouldn't pee myself and that if I did he wouldn't see it. I tried to remember what he looked like in order to help the authorities, but I couldn't. I could remember basically what we had said to one another, but the description of him was gone. Maybe I was focusing so much on what I had to do to get out of there with my cranium and jewelry intact that the details of his face were not important at the time.

I am not necessarily recommending this type of faking; I just know it worked for me that night under those circumstances. If he had been closer to me, I probably would have tried to run away or given up because I think physically I was overmatched.

20
Heroes: I Think I Can, I Think I Can

"Oh my garsh, I surprised myself and a few other people. I couldn't believe how I opened the door, how quick my mind worked."
—Karen Caylor, who dove into a Florida canal to rescue a woman trapped in a submerged car

On September 11, 2001, office workers Michael Benfante and John Cerqueira performed a minor miracle. With buildings collapsing and smoke choking the corridors of the North Tower at the World Trade Center in New York, Benfante and Cerqueira carried a wheelchair-bound woman down sixty-eight flights of stairs and freed her, minutes before the building collapsed.

"I could feel the building swaying," said Benfante, thirty-six, who had been working at his desk when a hijacked plane slammed into the tower, just eight floors above him. As Benfante, a former altar boy in the Catholic church, and co-worker Cerqueira, twenty-two, both five feet eleven inches and less than two hundred pounds, scrambled down the stairs, they came across a stranger struggling in a wheelchair. "Nobody was doing anything to help her," said Benfante. "In the back of my head, I could hear my mother telling me to get the heck out of there," Cerqueira said. "But I had to help."

The two men strapped the woman into a special chair in the stairwell for emergencies and carried her down the stairs, step by exhausting step.

Thousands of people from the tower would die that day. "When we got down to the lobby, it looked like Iwo Jima," said Cerqueira, whose ankle was injured.

People like those two businessmen, who attempt to save others from harm, offer us many lessons. If we study their actions, we can learn much about how to cope with a physical crisis, in particular how to deal with our emergency fear system.

One of the most important lessons—besides the character, unselfishness, and empathy that rescuers display—is how they overcome the initial fear of jumping into the fray when danger is all around them. Throughout a crisis, fear may come and go in waves, but the biggest fear of all is about getting involved. It may be a little like people who are afraid to go to the dentist or the doctor: their fear of going is actually greater than the real fear of getting hurt. Once they make the decision to go, their fear subsides considerably.

People who get involved in a crisis may have better control over their emergency fear system than the victims—and certainly more than the bystanders who choose not to get involved. By deciding to take action, they quickly remove one of the biggest distractions to success: their own fear of the situation. And in doing so, their focus seems automatically to improve.

Throughout this book we have seen that intense focus is key to overcoming pressure situations. Not only does focus on the task remove distractions and shift our mind-body chemistry away from debilitating fear, it can channel our survival hormones in the right direction and give us heightened awareness and physical powers.

"Concentrated attention can do some pretty amazing things," says Temple University psychology professor Frank Farley, who has studied heroism for years. "The sheer act of overcoming one's fear is a great feat in itself. After that, your concentration on the task increases. All your energy becomes concentrated on the crisis and you can perform some amazing things."

Office manager Bruce Dobbs reported abnormal powers as soon as he decided to help a man in a sinking car on a cold December day in 1987. Running in shorts and a T-shirt along the banks of the Potomac River in Arlington, Virginia, Dobbs saw a compact car speed off a highway and become airborne before splashing into the river. Immediately, Dobbs made the decision to rescue the drowning man. "I couldn't just stand there and watch this guy drown." For a second or two, Dobbs surveyed the scene. "As I stood at the bank, I remember thinking through the whole process, what I was going to do, jumping into the water, swimming seventy-five feet to the car, and pulling him out. It all came to me in a very few seconds. The analysis was vivid."

Dobbs, a father of three, carried out his actions to the tee, even though the cold water was "debilitating ... it was very difficult to breathe. I had to do it in short, ragged gasps." When he got to the sinking car, the driver would not get out; he just stared straight ahead. With uncommon strength, Dobbs got his fingers under the glass window and pulled so hard it broke, allowing him to grab the victim by the collar and yank him from the water-logged vehicle, even though the uncooperative man outweighed him by twenty pounds. Both suffered from hypothermia.

Like Dobbs, heroes often overcome their initial fear by not worrying too much about the potential harm if they do get involved, Farley says. "Generally, they act before they think, as opposed to thinking before they act."

After he was awarded the Bravery Star for saving a teenage girl from a rape in 1998, seventy-seven-year-old Bruce Butler of Napier, New Zealand, said his action was instinctive. "I'd do it again as long as I didn't have time to think about it."

I am not recommending that you jump into an impossible situation from which you cannot extricate yourself or the victims. Of course, you must assess a situation before you get involved. Like Bruce Dobbs, you need a very brief period of neutral observation before tackling the crisis. But know this: once you decide to get involved, you have overcome much of your own fear, and there are resources at your command that you may not realize you possess. Farley says that some people may shy away from helping at an automobile accident or during an assault because they are afraid, but also because they underestimate their own ability to help. "Fight or flight is wired into all of us. It's primitive and basic and very powerful."

Newspaper and police reports are full of stories of bystanders who don't get involved. Sometimes rescuers use their anger at such apathy as an added catalyst, as telephone-line technician Paul Ward did to free a woman from her crushed vehicle in Seven Hills, Australia, in 1999. Scilla Norris was hanging upside down in the wreck of her car, as a stream of gasoline flooded the smoking vehicle, but about thirty people stood and watched. "It made me really angry that nobody wanted to help," Ward recalls. He wrestled the mangled front door open, freed the dazed woman from her damaged seatbelt, and pulled her to safety. Ward's alliance of emotions was *fear-to-anger-to-action*.

Trigger Emotions

Instead of using anger as a trigger to overcome fear and dive into action, many rescuers use empathy for the victims. They briefly put their own lives on hold, making their unspoken formula for success *fear-to-empathy-to-dispassion*. "They seem to have an empathy for other people which spurs them on to risk their lives in the face of danger," says Walter Rutkowsky, executive director of the Carnegie Hero Fund Commission in Pittsburgh, which annually gives awards to Canadian and American heroes and heroines. Either they were born with empathy or they were taught it. "I think other people, particularly their parents, have taught them to have strong character."

In 1980, teenager Robert Noble, who was raised by a strict Mason family, climbed into a burning car to try to rescue four unconscious people in Fredonia, New York—despite pleas from his friends that it was too dangerous and that he might get sued if the rescue backfired. "I got angry," Noble recalled. "Somebody was dying and these are the things people think about!"

Noble saved the life of a woman, but a man died in his arms. (Throughout the rescue, Noble experienced heightened strength and concentration: "It seemed like I was all over the place at the same time.")

On March 7, 2001, Brent Paucke, a fourteen-year-old with Boy Scout training, took action to save his classmates—even when the school principal stood back as a screaming teenaged girl opened fire in the crowded cafeteria of Bishop Neumann Junior-Senior High School in Williamsport, Pennsylvania. The distraught girl shot another girl in the shoulder with a .22-caliber pistol and screamed: "Everybody get down!"

When freshman Paucke approached the shooter, the principal told Paucke to stay away. "The principal told me to get back, but you could tell she [the shooter] was really mad and she looked like she was about to go off on everybody," he said. "I didn't want anybody to get hurt."

As other students ran and hid under tables in fear, Paucke said he kept cool by keeping his mind blank except for what he would say to the girl. "I felt real scared, but I was saying, 'You don't have to do this. It doesn't have to be like this. It can be better. Just put the gun down or give it to me.' I tried to stay calm. If I sounded too upset, she might go off." Tears flowed down the girl's cheeks and, when she dropped the weapon, Paucke kicked it away. She was arrested.

Rescuers are often risk-takers by nature who also seek out adrenaline-increasing situations in their jobs and hobbies, Frank Farley says. "Often they have shown propensity to take risks in the past. The big moment comes along and they are ready for it. But I wish I understood them better because we need much more of this kind of heroism."

Other people have deep-seated needs to prove themselves. David Mayes told me he was not a fighter as a child. "Growing up, I can remember having a fight twice and I got my butt kicked both times." His family's instability (his father divorced twice) caused him sleeplessness. "I used to lie awake in bed and dream about becoming a hero. I'd dream about pushing someone out of the way of an oncoming car."

Mayes's chance for glory came on November 20, 1991, in Pasadena, Texas. Mayes, a video-store manager and father of three, was leaving a day-care center when he saw a man stabbing a woman. He fought with the attacker and experienced unusual concentration, quickness, and absence of pain despite being stabbed twice (once in the throat) with a kitchen knife. The attacker was arrested. "I can't believe that somebody else confronted with the same situation wouldn't react in the same way," Mayes says.

The Little Engine That Could

Feats of courage and physical prowess under duress have been reported by women and men, young and old. Here are a few examples:

- In Puyallup, Washington, on January 26, 1993, five-year-old Augustin Tudela Jr. held his three-year-old brother's head above icy water for ten minutes before their mother could reach them in a frozen pond.
- John Nesbitt, a sixty-six-year-old grandfather, got his adrenaline up to tackle and subdue a gunman holding his family hostage in their Calgary home in 1989.
- Five-year-old Rocky Lyons saved his mother Kelly's life on Halloween in 1987. Their pickup truck overturned down an embankment in Alabama. Kelly was badly cut (later needing 200 stitches) and could have bled to death. But the four-foot-tall, 60-pound Rocky pushed his five-foot-four, 104-pound mother out of the truck and back up the bank in the dark. As

she faltered, the boy reminded her of the story of *The Little Engine That Could*. "Remember, Mommy, I think I can, I think I can."

- Despina Buhagiar, a fifty-six-year-old homemaker, rescued Wendy Teather from being stabbed by an attacker in the kitchen of her home in St. Catharines, Ontario, on March 21, 1987. Buhagiar heard screams, entered her neighbor's house, and forced the man out the door with a baseball bat.
- In London, Ontario, in 1997, thirty-nine-year-old housekeeper Teresina Batikayo stopped a man from stabbing another man by pinning the attacker's arms behind him, forcing him to drop the knife.
- In Hope, British Columbia, in 1999, forty-three-year-old homemaker Myra Baloun defeated a cougar with a branch as it was mauling a young girl.
- Kemrey Magnant, a twenty-seven-year-old lumber yard assistant, pulled a woman who outweighed her from a car in Williston, Vermont, just before it became engulfed in flames.

In these cases, the rescuers not only overcame their initial fear, but also focused intently on the process of what they were doing. In the introduction to this book, I told how I swam across a swimming pool to help my wife Jennifer, who was unconscious and face-down. I think my success was due to pouring my fear energy into my arms and legs for stronger swimming strokes. I think I was able to remove the distraction of the terrible danger by recalling my experience in pressure situations at work.

Successful Rescuers ...

- make a decision to get involved, despite their fears.
- quickly go over in their mind what has to be done.
- sometimes use anger or empathy as triggers to get into the action.
- focus on what has to be done, not on the danger.
- report heightened focus, strength, quickness, speed, and willpower.

SUGGESTED READING

BOOKS ON FEAR
Fear Itself. Rush W. Dozier Jr., St. Martin's, 1998.
The Gift of Fear. Gavin de Becker, Dell, 1997.

BOOKS ON WORRY
Connect. Edward M. Hallowell, Pocket Books, 2001.
Worry. Edward M. Hallowell, Ballantine, 1997.

BOOKS ON STRESS
The Complete Idiot's Guide to Managing Stress. Jeff Davidson, Alpha, 1999.
Don't Sweat the Small Stuff. Richard Carlson, Hyperion, 1997.
The Relaxation Response. Herbert Benson, Avon, 1975.
Stress Management for Dummies. Allen Elkin, IDG Books, 1999.

BOOKS ON EMOTIONS
Anger: The Misunderstood Emotion. Carol Tavris, Touchstone, 1989.
The Emotional Brain. Joseph Le Doux, Simon and Schuster, 1996.
Intelligent Emotion. Frances Wilks, Arrow, 1998.
The Origin of Everyday Moods. Robert E. Thayer, Oxford, 1996.
Working with Emotional Intelligence. Daniel Goleman, Bantam, 1998.

BOOKS ON FEAR MANAGEMENT IN BUSINESS
Aerodynamic Trading. Constance Brown, New Classics, 1995.
The Corporate Athlete. Jack Groppel, Wiley, 2000.
Fight Your Fear and Win. Don Greene, Broadway, 2001.
Only the Paranoid Survive: How to Exploit the Crisis Points That Challenge Every Company. Andrew Grove, Bantam, 1999.
Stress for Success. James E. Loehr, Random House, 1997.

BOOKS ON PHOBIAS
The Anxiety and Phobia Workbook. Edmund J. Bourne, New Harbinger, 1995.
Facing Fears. Ada P. Kahn and Ronald M. Doctor, Checkmark, 2000.
Free Yourself from Fear. Valerie Austin, Thorsons, 1998.

BOOKS ON FOCUS

Finding Flow. Mihaly Csikszentmihalyi, Basic, 1997.

Flow: The Psychology of Optimal Experience. Mihaly Csikszentmihalyi, Harper and Row, 1990.

Index